"To have taken on a very public identity as a minority within a minority – in a community where lesbians are in danger of being raped and murdered is brave indeed. This is not to say that bravery in itself is compelling – it is the revealing of intimate details and private anguish, seldom discussed and sometimes awkwardly expressed, that makes this story worth reading."

Maureen Isaacson, *The Sunday Independent*

"A triumph of plain-speaking, all the more remarkable for its author having grown up in an atmosphere of 'secrecy and superstition'... The search for identity is a strong focus of the book and Nkabinde's story highlights the fact that all of us are, to varying degrees, the product of multiple and shifting identities."

Sharon Dell, *The Witness*

"What exactly makes a story about a lesbian sangoma notable? Is it the fact that it is about a sangoma or about a lesbian? Could it be the fact that we never discuss a sangoma's sexual orientation? Are sangomas even allowed to have sex? The reality is that this is a story about a woman like any other who, because of her life choices, is pushing the social boundaries of many South Africans."

Sihle Dlamini, *The Times*

"Nkunzi has made an astonishing breakthrough for homosexuality in Africa, because she has been accepted for who she is by standing up for lesbian and gay rights while completely retaining African culture."

Elspeth Bezemer-Mendes, *Tonight*

Black Bull, Ancestors and Me
My Life as a Lesbian Sangoma

Black Bull, Ancestors and Me
My Life as a Lesbian Sangoma

Nkunzi Zandile Nkabinde

The
ATLANTIC
Philanthropies

GALA

Hivos

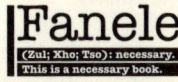

First published by Fanele – an imprint of Jacana Media (Pty) Ltd in 2008
Reprinted in 2009

10 Orange Street
Sunnyside
Auckland Park 2092
South Africa
+2711 628 3200
www.jacana.co.za

© GALA: 2008
© Cover photograph: Suzy Bernstein

All rights reserved.

ISBN 978-1-920196-06-6

Cover design by Jacana Media
Set in Stempel Garamond 11/15pt
Printed and bound by Pinetown Printers
Job No. 001050

See a complete list of Jacana titles at www.jacana.co.za

Acknowledgements

This book has been a dream for a long time. There are many people to thank for helping to make my dream come true. Firstly, my thanks go to Melody Emmett for helping me to tell my story. Next, I want to thank my family, especially my mother Sibongile Nkabinde, for the inspiration she gave me when she was alive and still gives me now; my sisters Thuli and Ntombi, for their friendship and support over the years; and my little brother Linda, for beating the drum for me.

Without my "second mother", Ruth Morgan from GALA, this book would not have been possible. For all the ways that she has supported and encouraged me since 2002, I am truly grateful.

Thanks to the sponsors and to Jacana Media, especially to Caroline Smith for her interest and advice.

Thanks to my trainer and to Hlengiwe, the sangoma from KZN who has taught me so much.

Contents

Life and Death 1

A Child in Two Worlds 14

Out and About 31

Following the Light 39

Remembering the Ancient Paths 52

Finding the Balance 67

In Search of Community 77

The Ancestors Don't Mind 121

Doing Things Differently 132

Hate Crimes 143

Making Connections 150

Glossary 160

CHAPTER ONE

Life and Death

Abe sekunjalo kakhulu
(Lo! It is now well so)

Abe sengingu Nkunzi Emnyama
(Lo! I am now Black Bull)

Insizwa yakwa Sangweni
(The young man of Sangweni)

Abe sekunjalo kakhulu
(Lo! It is now well so)

Abe sengidabuka ngenjabulo
(Lo! I now originate with joy)

Phezukomsebenzi wama khehla
(Upon the work of men)

Abe sekunjalo kakhulu
(Lo! It is now well so)

Abe sengithanda ukudumisa uyise wami
(Lo! I now love to glorify my father)

Abesengizalwa ngu Elemina
(Lo! I am now born of Elemina)

Insizwa yakwa muNsipa
(The young man of Nsipa)

Abe sekunjalo kakhulu
(Lo! It is now well so)

Abesekuba umkhulu uMahlasela
(Lo! There is now grandfather Mahlasela)

Insizwa Kadumase
(The young man of Dumase)

Abe sekunjalo kakhulu
(Lo! It is now well so)

Abesekuba umkhulu Dungamazi
(Lo! There is now grandfather Dungamazi)

Insizwa kaHlatshwayo
(The young man of Hlatshwayo)

Abe sekunjalo kakhulu
(Lo! It is now well so)

Abese kuba ngugogo Thumba
(Lo! There is now grandmother, Thumba)

Insizwa kaMcobokazi
(The young man of Mcobokazi)

Abe sekunjalo kakhulu
(Lo! It is now well so)

Abesekuba ngugogo Mkhulu Manza
(Lo! There is now great grandmother Manza)

Abese kuba inyoni elimhlophe lihlezi phezu kwamalwandle
(Lo! There is now a white bird sitting upon the oceans)

Abese kuba idada lidabula amanzi ngezimpiko
(Lo! There is now a duck cutting the water with its wings)

Abe sekunjalo kakhulu
(Lo! It is now well so)

Abese ngithanda uku nanazela abanikazi bempande
(Lo! I love to applaud the givers of the root)

Bona abangidabula ikhanda
(They who mend my head)

Bangivula isifuba
(They open my chest)

Ngisho impande ka Majoye
(I say the root of Majoye)

Abesekunjalo kakhulu
(Lo! It is now well so)

Abese ngithanda ukunanazela abanikazi bempande
(Lo! I now love to applaud the givers of the root)

THIS IS A PRAISE POEM to my ancestor, Nkunzi. Nkunzi is the ancestor who called me and gave me his name.

My name is Nkunzi. I am a Zulu woman, a lesbian, and a sangoma. This is my story.

I was born in Soweto, six months before the students protested about apartheid education and held the June 16th march in 1976. Soweto was tense in those days. There were police everywhere. Life was stressful and people were fed up. At night there was toyi-toying in the street outside the hostel in Meadowlands where my parents stayed. Today that hostel is an ordinary Soweto house but in those days each room was rented out to people who came from KwaZulu-Natal (KZN) and other parts of the country to look for jobs.

When my mother was pregnant with me, people said she was definitely going to give birth to a boy. They could tell because her face became so ugly. My parents already had two daughters, my sisters, Thembisile and Thulisiwe, so my father wanted a son to carry forward his name. My mother was expecting a boy. She had no idea she was going to bring twins into the world.

In the Zulu tradition, twins are unlucky. Before the time of Shaka they used to kill one baby if there were twins. It was not the first time for twins in my mother's family. My mom was one of eight children. Four passed away when they were still babies, including twin girls. In my father's family, there were no twins. The Nkabinde clan does not allow twins. They are not accepted. Twins die in the Nkabinde family.

My father was a truck driver and he was often away. He was not around when my mother's labour pains started. My mother had a friend at the hostel, Mamtshali, who was also pregnant. When Mamtshali heard my mom calling, she ran to assist her. Immediately she saw that my mother was in labour, so she rushed outside to look for transport to the clinic. The police stopped her and asked for her dompas. She told them she didn't have it with her because she was in a hurry to find transport for a pregnant woman inside the hostel. Without listening to what she was saying they shoved Mamtshali into the back of the police van.

A neighbour saw what happened and he drove my mother to the clinic in Zone 4 in Meadowlands. She found Mamtshali already there. The police had pushed her so hard that she was also in labour. It was too soon for Mamtshali's baby to be born so he was dead when he arrived.

My brother was the first born. Like Mamtshali's baby, he was also dead when he came out. I came a few minutes after my twin brother and I survived. I was born just before midnight on 7 December 1975.

The same neighbour who took my mother to the clinic phoned my father's employer and my father raced back to Meadowlands as soon as he heard the news. By the time he arrived at the clinic there had been two deaths in my family: my grandmother from my father's side of the family and my mother's uncle both died on the day that I was born.

My grandmother was living in Piet Retief at the time of her death. She and my grandfather had separated after my grandfather, who was an important person in the Church of Zion in Meadowlands, began to have an affair with a woman from the congregation. My grandmother begged him to leave this woman but he refused. My grandmother died of a heart attack but I can't help thinking that she probably had a broken heart as well.

After hearing about my grandmother's death, my grandfather was so stubborn he refused to collect her body, so her brothers buried her in Piet Retief as if she was a woman who had never married and never had children.

My mother's Uncle Gnevusa from KZN also died. He died on the day I was born. He was a handsome man and a ladies' man like my grandfather. He had seven wives and many girlfriends. The story in the family is that he was poisoned. His throat started to swell after a jealous man gave him some bad fruit. His family took him to the hospital and to traditional healers but nothing helped. The infection spread from his throat to his chest and his skin turned grey. He also died on 7 December 1975, my birthday.

My father named me Beauty, after his mother. My grandmother didn't have a Zulu name. My mom gave me the name Zandile, which means "increase". She said, "I have given birth to a daughter instead of a son and two members of the family have died. The problems in the family have increased."

My mother always reminded me that I was born with death all around me. She used to forget the dates when my brothers and sisters were born but she never forgot the date of my birthday because of all the deaths on that day.

When my father drove back to the hostel with my mother and me, a woman who was a prophet from the Church of Zion was waiting for us. My father was a member of the Zion church and he knew this woman. She spoke to my father and said: "Don't

LIFE AND DEATH

take this child to your father's house because if you take her there, she is going to die." My father asked her, "Why?" She said, "In your family, do twins survive?" My father said, "No, they don't survive."

I was the first twin to live in my father's family. I think I survived because my ancestors knew I had something to do for them. Maybe when I was still in my mother's womb they knew I had been chosen to be a healer and that is why I lived. When my father heard the prophet's warning, he paid attention because in that moment he knew that it was the ancestors speaking.

My father asked the woman, "What shall I do?" And she said, "You had better take this child to your wife's family's side." That same night my mom and dad drove from Soweto to *isigodi sikaKhanyile* – the home of the Khanyile clan near Empangeni in KZN.

I grew up without knowing that I was a twin. It was a family secret. Long after my parents died I asked my aunt what happened when I was born. She didn't want to talk about it either. She said, "Nobody wants to open up that wound." She was afraid to reveal my mother's secrets. She said my dead mother could not defend herself in the world of the living so it was not right to interfere in her business, but I had to know the truth so I begged her until she agreed to tell me what happened.

There has always been secrecy and superstition in my family. Even when I was a young child my parents were full of thoughts and emotions that they never expressed. When you don't know what is going on inside people close to you it makes you nervous and you expect the worst to happen.

After hearing the news about my twin brother, I started to think about how my life would be different if he had lived. Maybe I wouldn't even be gay. I wished I could ask my mom,

7

"If you could have made a choice, who would you have chosen?" And I remembered a story she told me when I was growing up about a fight with my father when she was pregnant with me. She told me my father hit her in her stomach. Sometimes when I feel sad and alone, I think that maybe my father didn't want me to live, although I know this is not true because he loved me when I was a baby. My father's problems with my mother were nothing to do with me or my brothers and sisters but he had a way of turning against all of us if he was angry with my mother.

When I was a child growing up I always felt that a part of me was missing. In December near my birthday, I start to become numb. It just happens. I become restless. I can't feel anything because my body becomes so heavy. Now I know that this is because my twin brother is trying to get closer to me. His spirit was awake in me all these years and I never understood that before. I didn't know that I had another part of me that passed away. My brother loves to praise. If my twin brother's spirit is in me, I feel like praising. He is full of joy and energy. When I am dancing, if I am in a ceremony, he has his songs, his praises. When Nkunzi gives other ancestors in me a space, my brother will come and sing his praises.

My mother's family welcomed us in KZN. My father waited three days before driving back to Johannesburg because he wanted to hold me in his arms. Zulu men are not allowed to hold a baby until the umbilical cord has fallen out. My aunt says even when I was a baby I resembled my father and he was very proud.

* * *

Life and Death

I was introduced to my mother's ancestors when I was one year and six months of age. I was nearly a teenager when I was introduced to my father's ancestors.

My mother held me in her arms and my parents and elders from my mother's family took me to the family graveyard. Two chickens – a cock and a hen – were sacrificed for my male and female ancestors from my mother's family. My uncle and an elderly relative spoke to the ancestors, informing them that I was a child of those parts and that my father was from the Nkabinde clan. My uncle called on the ancestors to open up the path in front of me and teach me the ways of my clan. Afterwards, a celebration was held. A goat was slaughtered and a feast was prepared for my family and for neighbours from all around. A bracelet made from the goat's hair – *isiphandla* – was tied around my left wrist, the side for my mother. Some months later, when the ancestors had settled in me, the bracelet fell off on its own. That was the sign that the ancestors were happy that I had taken my place in the family.

* * *

My grandmother from my mother's side died long before I was born. She was from the MacKenzie clan. Her family members were Khoisan people and they came to Johannesburg from the Cape and her ancestors were with the first people who came to South Africa. My grandmother was named Zalusile and her other name was Gertrude. In those days, most African people had a traditional name and an English or Afrikaans name because white employers needed a name they could pronounce. She was light in complexion and she spoke Afrikaans. She had her own house in Sophiatown. That was the time when African people were allowed to own a house in places like Sophiatown and Newclare. Sophiatown is famous because it was a mixed area where different cultures and languages mixed together. Africans, coloureds, Indians and Chinese all lived together.

My grandmother had the gift of healing and of prophecy. She worked as a domestic worker first and then she became a vendor after she had a vision and God told her she must not work for a white master any more. She sold all kinds of goods: things to eat, household goods, and clothes. She bought and sold whatever she could manage to make a profit. I suppose today she would be called an entrepreneur. She was a single mom most of the time and she found a way to survive. My grandmother was also a prophet and a healer in the community. Because of her work on the streets, everybody knew her and they knew about her healing powers and her passion for everything to do with the Church of Zion. She had that spiritual way about her, the same as me.

When the government started forcing people to move, my grandmother met with other prophets and they prayed night and day. The people were shouting, *"Ons dak nie, ons phola hier"* (We won't move). But the police came from Meadowlands police station with guns and police vans and they took many, many people to Meadowlands, Lenasia, Western Coloured Township and Noordgesig.

My grandmother ran away to a house at 136 South Avenue in Newclare with her four children, including my mother. The houses in Newclare were small and overcrowded. There were four rooms in Number 136 and in each room a different family was living. Next door to the room where my mother lived there was an Indian family. The room had a single bed which was balanced on top of paint tins because my grandmother was superstitious and wanted to protect herself from the *tokoloshe* (evil spirit), and there was one wardrobe.

When we were growing up, our elders told us that there is utokoloshe, who goes around stealing children. They would tell us that if utokoloshe comes, we should go and hide under the bed. For them, to lift up the bed was to make space for us kids to hide.

But that is not the truth. The truth is that it was a space to put our sponge when we woke up in the morning; there wasn't enough space in the house.

Life was very hard in Newclare. Everyone was poor. People were not friendly to one another like they were in Sophiatown. There was fighting between street gangs and there was a lot of crime. Women brewed beer to make enough money to survive so there were always drunk people in the streets and always police arresting people for no reason. It was a dangerous place to live.

My grandmother gave birth to eight children but four died, including twin girls. My mother's name was Sibongile. She was also called Olga. She was born after the twins girls who died and before her sister, Notsokolo, who also died. She was born with death around her, like me. The youngest living child in the family was my aunt, Ntombi. My mother and my Aunt Ntombi had the same father. My grandfather on my mother's side was from Newcastle in KZN. My grandmother never married him but he accepted my mother and my Aunt Ntombi as his children. When I was 14, my mom took us to meet my grandfather. He welcomed us and there was a ceremony at the family cemetery to introduce us to the elders who were buried there. I have always felt connected to those ancestors.

After some time, my mom and her family were moved to Meadowlands. Today there are a few trees in Meadowlands and the roads are tarred but in those days it was a dry, dusty place with no trees. They moved into a long, thin, Meadowlands hostel which is now the house where my Aunt Zodwa still lives today.

My grandmother was bitten by a dog and the wound went poisonous. Because she was a prophet, she knew about her death before it happened. One day she told the members of her church that she had a vision of a large congregation with people from all different churches gathering together on the 25th of September to pay their respects to somebody who had died. The 25th September was the day of her own funeral and it was exactly as she described it.

Zodwa was already working when my grandmother died in 1969 so she became the one to support the younger children in the family, including my mother. When my mother was 21 she married my father and got pregnant with my sister, Ntombi. My mom and dad met at the Mzimvubu School in Meadowlands, where my sisters and I also went to school. Zodwa says my father was so neat and good looking but the family was not sure about him because he was so dark skinned. They said he looked like a man from another country in Africa but my mother loved him and she didn't care about his dark complexion.

✳ ✳ ✳

The Nkabinde family came from the Piet Retief area near the border of Swaziland in Mpumalanga but my father was born in Meadowlands and he grew up there. There were eight children in my father's family as well. My father's name was Mathew and he was the oldest son. All my uncles except the youngest one, my uncle Ray, have died. One uncle died of cancer; one was murdered in Mfolo; one disappeared; and one died of AIDS. My father's two sisters, my aunts Gabisele and Thabisile are still living. My grandfather is also still alive. He is a very old man now and he lives in the same house in Meadowlands where my father grew up. This house was also a home to me when I was growing up.

* * *

When I think about my life, I realize that I felt the presence of my ancestors at a young age. They were always with me. I have been told that twins have special powers for communicating with *Amadlozi*[1] and with each other. Now I understand that my twin brother died because otherwise I was going to die. Something happened in my mother's womb so that only one of us could survive and my ancestors saw that it had to be me because of the work I am supposed to do to bring healing to the family and to the community. It is a mystery that I will only understand completely when I cross over to the other side. My brother is still communicating with me in my spirit. The relatives who died on the day I was born also gave me their spirits when they died. They gave me spiritual power to become a healer.

---

1 Ancestors

CHAPTER TWO

A Child in Two Worlds

I WAS TWO-MONTHS-OLD when my mother left me with her aunt and uncle in KZN. I called them *ugogo* and *umkhulu*[1] but they were my great aunt and great uncle. The farm had many thatched roof huts made of cow dung and mud. There were separate huts for girls and boys but when I was a baby I stayed with my great aunt and she took care of me. *Mielies* (maize) and sugar cane were plentiful and there was a dam where my girl cousins went to do the washing and collect water. Not far away there was the family graveyard where the elders went to communicate with the ancestors.

My mother was a domestic worker in Johannesburg and she came to visit when she could. Sometimes she took me back to Meadowlands with her for some weeks or months for a visit. When I was two I was playing with my uncle Ray, the fifth child in my father's family, in the front yard of the house. By that time, my parents were renting a house in Meadowlands. Suddenly, the police arrived and wanted to arrest my uncle. Without thinking, he picked me up and used me as a human shield. One of the policemen wanted to shoot and the other one said, "Don't shoot

---

1   Grandmother and grandfather

the baby." Instead, the policeman tried to hit my uncle with the back of his gun. Accidentally, he hit the side of my head and the blood started to flow. I still have that scar, even today.

When he saw the blood, my uncle Ray threw me at the policeman and ran away. My mother came running out shouting, "My child! My child!" The policeman handed me to my mom and chased after my uncle with the other policeman in the van. My father also came out and started shouting at my mother, "I told you to leave this child in KZN. Why did you bring her here?" So there was that conflict already between my parents.

After that incident, my uncle managed to escape. He went into exile as a member of the ANC.[2] My parents never spoke about politics. They didn't teach us anything about politics. They talked about the church and about culture and ancestors but there was no talk about politics. Sometimes they used to wonder what had happened to my uncle Ray and where he was when they watched TV, but they never talked about the ANC or anything to do with politics.

In 1989 one of my Uncle Ray's friends arrived with a letter and that is how we knew he was still alive but we didn't see him again until he came back to the country in 1997. I didn't remember him because I was a baby the last time I had seen him. He asked me, "Don't you know me?" And I said, "No, I don't know you." He said, "Do you know about this scar on your head?" And I said, "No." And he told me the story of how I got this scar. He wasn't embarrassed about what he did. He said he knew the policeman wouldn't shoot a baby.

* * *

---

2 African National Congress

After some time my great uncle died and my mother's brother, Vusumuzi, took over the homestead in KZN. He was my favourite uncle. He taught me about Zulu culture and to love the land and to respect everything about life in a rural area. That respect is still in me. I loved it in the country. I loved the way of life. My uncle taught me to recognise the birds and how to tell from the sounds they make when it will rain.

My uncle had a kraal full of cattle. He called each one by name. There was one cow called Umbona, which means "reddish-coloured skin" and another called Mahlabahlabane, meaning "sharp horns". Another was named Romano. She was so sweet. There was a church next door, the church of the Romans.[3] She normally liked to go and sleep there when she was a calf. That is why they called her Romano. I loved that cow.

There was also a hunting dog with the name *Intombiyebhayi*.[4] My uncle took Intombiyebhayi with him when he went hunting. She was so clever, she could smell a rabbit from far away and she always caught it when my uncle set her free.

I used to share my food with this dog when I was a young child. My aunt would prepare soft porridge and I would eat half and Intombiyebhayi would eat the other half from the same bowl.

My uncle named this dog Intombiyebhayi because she didn't have puppies. My uncle said she was like a virgin doing the reed dance. The reed dance is the traditional dance that girls perform when they go for *ukuhlolwa*.[5]

My uncle Vusumuzi respects all the traditions that are part of Zulu culture and I grew up with this respect. Even now I have

---

3 Roman Catholic Church
4 Maiden or virgin
5 Virginity testing

this respect in me. Sometimes I feel tense inside because what I was taught about Zulu culture as a child in KZN is in conflict with what I have learned from growing up and living the life of a lesbian in Meadowlands. For example, there is a part of me that believes in virginity testing. My ancestor, Nkunzi, also influences my beliefs. For Nkunzi, virginity testing is a way of keeping Zulu culture alive. Nkunzi believes in keeping power in the hands of the elders because they are the ones who know what is best for everyone in the community.

When I look around at the young girls of these days who are getting pregnant by different fathers at the age of 14 or 16 or 18, and when I see the way that AIDS is spreading like a fire in the youth, I understand what Nkunzi is seeing and I think that virginity testing could also be a good thing. Then on the other side I understand that because of our Constitution, girls have certain rights and virginity testing stands in the way of those rights. Because I have these different sides in me I can see the traditional way and the modern way; I can see the way of a Zulu man and I can see why some women – especially gender activists – have a problem with virginity testing. As a sangoma I am trained to see what is happening behind what we normally see so with virginity testing, I can see light in all sides and I can see the shadows in all sides. My life is not only for myself, it is also for my ancestors, especially my ancestor, Nkunzi.

In my tradition a girl who is in her menstruation time is not supposed to mix with others. The traditional way is for a girl who is menstruating to stay in a separate room until her menstruation time is over. In rural areas, if there are two girls menstruating, they will both be kept together in the room until their days are done. They are locked in the room until they have finished menstruating and then they will go to the dam and wash themselves. For some people this sounds like a punishment but for me it sounds like kindness and respect.

My period started during the day after my 18th birthday. We went to a Christmas party on Boxing Day at my uncle's place in Zone 6 in Meadowlands. Afterwards it was just me and my mom at home. I started to have cramps down below in my belly. When I went to the toilet I felt something hot and I saw the blood. I screamed and called my mom to come and see. I thought I was hurt.

My mother came and she said, "It is fine. Take a bath and come to me." Then she gave me a pad and told me to put it on my underwear. I did what she said but it made me feel so heavy. She wanted to see if I was able to walk with the pad so she sent me to my grandfather's house. As I was walking down the street she was looking at me. I was pressing my thighs together, afraid that this thing would fall. I felt so naked and so confused. I didn't know anything about menstruation even though I was 18. I used to hang out with boys and in my family, even my sisters only spoke to my mom about menstruation. They never told me about it. I saw the pads a few times by accident when I opened my mother's drawers but I never questioned her because in my family children were not allowed to ask my parents questions.

For five days I lay on top of my bed with terrible period pains and wanting to vomit all the time. My mother came and checked on me and gave me new pads as I needed them. After five days it stopped and my mother spoke to me and explained that now I was in the adult way and I must be careful because if I slept with a man I could fall pregnant and have a child. I told her, "I will never sleep with a man. Never."

When I menstruated I stayed indoors all the time. I wished I could switch off menstruation. I needed to stay away from other people because I didn't want anyone to see me. I washed all the time. I wanted to wash away the blood. It made me feel dirty.

Since I started to have the spirit of Nkunzi in me I hardly menstruate. I only menstruate when I have a female ancestor in me. With Nkunzi I can stay up to a year without menstruating. Even when I was in training I went for four or even six months without menstruating for more than a day. My trainer told me it was because my ancestor was a male and he had taken my menstruation away. Now I don't worry because I know that Nkunzi has cut off my feminine, menstruation side. If I am menstruating then I know that it is because a female spirit is in me. Although I love it when there is a female spirit in me, I have never learned to cope with menstruation or with having breasts. I hate breasts. I didn't want to have breasts. I have never bound my breasts but my breasts are a part of my body that I don't like. If I was rich, I would have an operation to remove my breasts.

* * *

I was happy in KZN. There were a lot of other children and I was never alone. The older boys would go out with a panga or an axe to get sugar cane. They would cut it into small sticks and put it in an *uqhwembe*[6] for the younger children. We would suck the sticks until there was no taste left and then throw them to one side for the birds. I wanted to go with the boys to fetch the sugar cane but they wouldn't allow it. They said there were snakes. When I was older I found out that the boys used to take their girlfriends into the sugar cane to make love to them there. That is why they didn't want the younger children to go with them.

---

6 Large bowl

Sometimes the boys would get up early in the morning, long before sunrise, and after finishing their tasks, they walked to the river, which was quite a long way away. There they would catch fish, including small fish which they put in tins for the younger children to play with. We used to wait for them to come back. We were always excited about what they would bring home from their trip to the river.

Although I enjoyed playing with the other children, I always wanted to be around my uncle Vusumuzi. I preferred his company to playing with the other children. My uncle didn't make me aware of the differences between girls and boys until I became a teenager. After that he told me about the different roles for boys and girls; like boys fight with sticks and girls sweep the yard. My uncle taught me about my culture in passing and I learned many things from following him and watching what he did. I learned what is expected of a Zulu girl and I learned about the life of a Zulu man. I was more interested in the life of a Zulu man. Some of the girls' things did not feel right for me. I remember I was told to drink warm milk from the cow so that I would grow up to be a healthy mother and give birth to healthy children. I had to struggle to drink that milk. I didn't like the taste and I didn't see myself as someone who would get pregnant and be the mother of children.

My uncle was different from most Zulu men because he had a gentle side and he was not afraid to show his emotion. One day Intombiyebhayi was found dead. Somebody had poisoned her. I cried and cried because I loved that dog and I knew my uncle loved her too.

My aunt beat me when I cried. She said, "Why are you crying for a dog?" I told her that I loved that dog and I went on crying until even some neighbours came, thinking that somebody in the family had passed away.

My uncle was also sad. They say in African culture that a man mustn't show his sorrow and he mustn't cry, but that day when I looked at him I saw in his face that he had lost something he loved. He didn't eat or speak that day. He went away and only came home at sunset. I felt his grief with my own grief. A long time afterwards when I asked him if he remembered that dog, his face started to change and I could see that it still made him sad to think of Intombiyebhayi.

* * *

When I was four my mother took me back to Meadowlands. It was hard for me to leave my uncle. I resisted going with my mother and she beat me. My uncle had never beaten me and he shouted at my mother, "Why are you doing that to her?" But I was my mother's child, so he could not stop her from taking me with her. To me it felt like I had been hijacked or kidnapped. This feeling stayed with me, even though I went back to visit my uncle in the Easter holidays and at Christmas. He missed me and I missed him. Even today I feel more free and more at home in KZN.

Life in Soweto was so different. Living in Meadowlands and in Empangeni was like living in two different countries. In KZN life was peaceful but in Soweto there was always fighting in the house. Even when there was no fighting the atmosphere was heavy because my parents were not happy. My mother never told us what was happening but you could see from her actions when there was fighting. Because of her ancestors my mother was light in her complexion so you could see if she was upset. Her skin would go red and her eyes would be red from crying.

She would send me and my sisters to my grandfather's house if she was fighting with my father. I didn't want to go and she would shout, "Go! Go!" If I didn't go, she would take out a belt to beat me, so I would run away. We would come back the next morning and I would see that her eyes were red and she hadn't had any sleep. If I asked her what was wrong, she said, "Nothing!" If I asked too many questions, she would shout at me to go away. It was not okay to ask your parents questions as a child. We didn't eat with my parents. My mother used to dish up for us and we sat on the floor in the kitchen. When we were finished my parents used to eat their food. We didn't sit with them. The way I was raised, children and adults didn't talk very much.

My mother used to punish us when we did wrong things like telling a lie or taking some of the coins she left on her dressing table. She didn't hit us when my father was around because he didn't allow it. She used to wait until he went away, then she would come into the bathroom when I was about to take a bath and take out the belt. I was naked and the door was locked so there was nothing I could do. For my older sisters it was worse because my mother used a cane which was much harder. After some time I knew that my mom was saving up the punishments for when my father was away, so I used to run to my grandfather's place and stay there until my father came back.

I think the reason why my mother was so strict was because if we did something wrong my father would make my mother take the blame. He expected my mother to give us guidance and if we went wrong, he said it was her fault. When my sister got pregnant when she was still at school, my father blamed my mother for not teaching her properly.

A Child in Two Worlds

* * *

I remember when I was a six or seven, I used to cry when my mom braided my hair. My hair was big and it was painful when she combed it, but when she was finished I looked beautiful and I felt so proud. My hair was pitch black and people loved it. They gave me sweets and they said to my mom, "Your child is an African beauty." I loved the attention. I enjoyed getting money and sweets from adults and I enjoyed people taking pictures of me because I was pretty. I remember I had a dress with flowers and a little jacket that went with it. At that time I loved being a little girl. Even now, I enjoy the times when I feel feminine. I become emotional and I show my emotions when I have a feminine spirit in me. This feminine side is still in me but it doesn't come out very often, except in my work as a healer.

As I grew older I turned into a tomboy. I enjoyed boys' games. I was forced to play with my sisters if they were around, but I preferred to play with boys. If my sisters were playing house and they needed a child for the game, I would have to be the child and I would become very bored. If I was playing house with my friends, I would always make sure I was the father of the house.

I wanted to be a truck driver like my father and I used to play truck games with boys from the neighbourhood. We also played marbles and soccer. I loved soccer. I became more and more of a tomboy and I <u>hated wearing dresses.</u>

My father's youngest brother, my Uncle Nkosnye, was training to be a policeman and he used to come and stay with us sometimes. I would steal his shorts and wear them under my tracksuit pants. They were too big but I used to tie them up with a belt. He would tell everyone, "I am missing some shorts," and I would just keep quiet. Then on Saturdays when my mother did the washing, I just mixed the shorts with the washing and my mother would say to my uncle, "I found your shorts. They were with the washing."

Sometimes, when my mother made me wear a dress, tears would come to my eyes because I felt so uncomfortable. It felt wrong to me. I felt I was not supposed to be wearing a dress. As soon as I could, I would change into jeans or shorts or a tracksuit. Then I felt I could go anywhere. My mom would nag me and tell me to stop being so rough. I wanted to tell her, my mom, that there is something in me that makes me like this and I am free when I am like this. I think Nkunzi was in this part of me even when I was growing up.

There was a big wooden box outside the house in Meadowlands. Sometimes my mother used it for storage and at other times it was empty. I used to play a game with some of the girls from the neighbourhood. I would take them into the box with a candle, pretending it was a house, but when we were inside in the dark, I would kiss them. The first time I did this, I was nine years old. We had a black and white TV at home and one day when all the elders were watching a programme called, *All My Children*, I went outside with one of the other girls. I took her to the box and when we were inside I started to kiss her. It felt nice.

Eventually when I played with girls I used to kiss them and then I wanted to touch them but I felt scared. I was just playing. I didn't know that I liked girls. I think my mom saw what was happening but she didn't want to talk about it.

When I was 11 I fell and hurt my arm when I was playing on an old car in my grandfather's backyard with my cousins and some boys from the neighbourhood. That night the pain was so bad I couldn't sleep and by the morning, my arm was swollen. I woke my grandfather and he called my father to take me to the hospital. I was discharged the next day with a plaster cast right the way up my arm. Three months later, a few days after the plaster was taken off, I was climbing a tree with the same boys when I fell again and broke the same arm. For the second time I had plaster on my arm.

Whenever my father returned from a long trip it was always exciting to see the big truck parked in the road outside the house and all the children used to come and climb onto it. I broke my arm for the third time when I slipped against the dashboard of the truck.

I saw the same doctor at Baragwanath hospital each time I broke my arm. The third time I saw him, he told my father to take me to a sangoma. The sangoma said my father must buy my grandmother's name because my grandmother had passed away on the day that I was born. So my father bought a goat and I went to my grandmother's grave with my parents and my grandfather to perform a ceremony there. My father performed a ritual with two chickens and some snuff and candles. Afterwards we went home and my father slaughtered the goat. Some white robes were placed over my head and *isiphandla* was tied around my wrist. There were no more accidents after that.

* * *

My father combined traditional beliefs and Christian beliefs. My mother never loved the church but she went to the Church of Zion because of my father, and she took me and my sisters with her. I remember I had to wear a blue and white dress. I hated it. It was a long walk to the church meeting and the service was for three hours, from 12 until three on a Sunday. I used to sleep most of the time because I was so bored.

Sometimes the elders in the church would tell my mother that she had a calling. My mom would start to roar and she would go into a trance and the elders would gather around her and try to work with her. They said she had a calling to be a prophet and a healer like my grandmother. My mother would become strong and brave when her ancestors were in her, but she couldn't see a way to follow the calling because she said she had to take care of her children. One day she stopped going to church so I stopped going too.

My father used to consult sangomas. He didn't tell us but we could see because of the herbs he brought home and sometimes he sent me to buy the herbs for him. Once he took the whole family to consult a sangoma. I was 16. I don't know what was happening in my family at that time but my parents were fighting about money. It was a long drive to Pretoria in my father's car and my mother was quiet the whole way. I could see she was not happy. The sangoma in that area was an old man. We took our shoes off before we entered his room. He prayed over the bones before throwing them and then he asked my father to put down some money. The door and the windows were closed but suddenly there was strong wind in the room. The wind took my father's money. After watching this, the man gave the money back to my father and told him to buy food for the house with it.

We were all quiet when we drove back to Johannesburg. When we got home my father didn't buy food. He took that same money and went to find another sangoma. On the way there he was hijacked and he lost the car and all the money he had.

Money was always short, especially when my father was away. Sometimes there was nothing to eat in the house and my mom used to tell us to drink warm water and go to bed. Once my mother lost her job and she couldn't pay the rent. My father was out of town and the police came to our house. My mother was fighting with them in Afrikaans so I couldn't understand what she was saying. My older sisters were standing there crying. The police pushed my mother out of the way and started taking everything out of the house. They were taking our things away because my parents hadn't been paying the rent. My mother ran to call my aunt and they packed everything and took it to my grandfather's house, which was just a few streets away from where we lived. My father found us there when he came back.

My grandfather's house had three rooms and some grass and flowers outside in the front. There was no fence and children from the neighbourhood used to come and visit. We stayed there for a couple of months. My parents had a shack outside in the yard. When my mother found another job, we moved back to the house without my father. My mom told us, "Your father wants to stay in your grandfather's house. He won't be coming to stay with us here." There were so many people staying in my grandfather's house. Every night everything in the kitchen had to be moved to one side so that my aunt and my uncle could sleep there. I couldn't understand why my father wanted to stay at my grandfather's place instead of coming home with us.

* * *

My grandfather was not a very talkative person. He didn't show me things like my uncle in KZN. He always wanted us to keep quiet, especially on Sundays. I remember he told us a story from the bible about a woman who always went to collect wood carrying her baby on her back. One day God appeared to her and said, "I have warned everyone that Sunday is a day of resting and you, you are working. I am taking you away and putting you in the moon." All the time when I looked up at the moon, I saw this woman carrying a baby on her back, with a bunch of wood on her head. So that woman, for me I felt that she was punished for working for her family, for trying to take her family wood. It made me think of my mom leaving early every morning to try and earn money to keep us alive.

My grandfather was a carpenter. He made chairs and tables and other furniture. He had a good job with a firm in town. He liked to gamble and he liked women. When he got paid he used to go to Dube to bet on the horses. If he won he would buy cold-drinks and peanuts for all the children. If he was not lucky he would just go into his room and keep quiet.

He was a pastor at the Zion church. He had a long white beard and on Saturdays he would put on his blue and white uniform and walk to the church with his wooden stick. He used to wash his handkerchief before going to church but instead of hanging it out to dry he would swing it around in his hand so that it was dry by the time he arrived at church, then he folded it and put it in his pocket.

When I stayed with my grandfather, all eight grandchildren slept on the floor on grass mats in his bedroom. One time when I was sleeping there, I felt somebody's heavy breath next to me. It was dark so I couldn't see who it was. I felt there was someone on top of me. At first I thought I was dreaming. Then I tried to move my hands and push whatever was on top of me away, but I couldn't. I tried to open my mouth but I couldn't. Then suddenly I just fell asleep again, as if I was collapsing. When I woke up I found that all the bottom part of my body was wet. I went and took a bath. I was so confused. The second time it happened I saw that it was my uncle Mandla. He covered my face with my nightdress. He was on top of me and he closed my mouth with his hand so I couldn't scream. I collapsed again. In the morning after taking a bath, I told my grandfather I missed my mother and I went back to my mother's place. I was 8-years-old and I was not in a clear light about my sexuality.

Another time after that, my mother left me with a neighbour. I think the woman went to the shops and left her son in the house. When I was sleeping he came and he lifted me up and put me on top of the bed and then he was on top of me too.

All these memories came back when I was already grown up and finished school. It was something that was inside me. It came back in pieces. I never told my mother or my sisters about it.

* * *

My father would go away and come back and when he was at home there was fighting. One day, my father called a meeting of all of us children. There were six of us by then, three girls and my three younger brothers. He told us he was divorcing my mother. He said we are not his family, not his children. My mom cried.

I said, "Look at me; I look like you. How can you say I am not your child?" He said, "You are not my child." After my father rejected us, life was very hard. I wanted to protect my mom, to help her. I hated to see her suffer.

My mother used to sit alone and talk to her ancestors or pray to God. She always used snuff before talking. If she didn't have her snuff we wouldn't sleep in the house. Sometimes she couldn't find where she had put it and she used to wake us up to help her find it. We used to go to a neighbour to borrow some if she ran out of snuff in the night because she couldn't sleep without it.

At times she would start talking in a different voice and her eyes would change. I would go out when she did this. I wasn't scared as much as disturbed. I grew up in a family that believed in ancestors and sangomas so I understood that my mother had a calling and my mother knew she had a calling but she put her family first and she didn't want to spend the money on the training.

Sometimes my mother would talk to her ancestors for a long time. I would hear deeper voices coming out of her but I couldn't understand what she was saying. It used to make me angry and I would leave the house. I think I must have known that she was ignoring the ancestors and not accepting her calling.

Now that I also use snuff when I talk to my ancestors, I understand more about what was happening with my mother. My ancestor, Nkunzi, couldn't express himself through my mother because she refused. My mother was not allowing him to come out.

CHAPTER THREE

Out and About

WHEN I WAS TEN, I went back to my uncle's place in KZN. I stayed there for three years and I was very happy. I didn't attend school that much because my uncle didn't believe that girls should have an education. Somebody in the family told my mother that I wasn't going to school and she came to fetch me. She had a fight with my uncle and she shouted at him, "Why don't you let her go to school? Why do you make me waste my money on the uniform?" My uncle had sold my uniform because he said there was no use in girls going to school. "She will just get married and have children so what is the use?"

I was crying when I left with my mother but I didn't have a choice. Once again I had to do what my mother said because she was my mother. I was angry and hurt for a long time. Now I realize that if I had stayed with my uncle I would have been uneducated and probably I would have been in an arranged marriage.

My uncle told me that I must learn to fight for myself and to look after myself. He used to say, "When you go back to Egoli, there are people who will try to touch you and do something to you. You must fight." He taught me how to protect myself from boys. When I was older and boys started to proposition me, I remembered what he said.

After coming back to Meadowlands I started to isolate myself. I became quiet.

At school I was falling back with my schoolwork and my teacher could tell that there was something wrong. She told my mother I was not concentrating and there was a problem.

There was this girl who was sharing a desk with me. When she touched me, I started to sweat. This was disturbing me. The teacher noticed and she told my mother but my mom didn't take it seriously. The teacher sent me to the social worker and the social worker wrote a letter telling my mother to take me to the counselling centre in town.

When we arrived there, my mother went in alone first and spoke to the social worker. Then I went in and my mother waited outside. After I closed the door, the social worker said, "You are beautiful." I turned around because I thought she was talking to someone behind me, so she said, "It is only you and me in this room." She told me to sit down and after a while she said, "Come here," so I went to her and she said, "Kiss me." I bent over and gave her a baby kiss and she grabbed me and kissed me. I couldn't believe what was happening to me. It was so wonderful. She told me I was a lesbian. I didn't know what a lesbian was but I knew that whatever it was, I wanted to be one. I was so happy. I felt I was in love.

She asked me, "Do you want to come and see me again?" I just nodded my head. There was so much going on in me, I didn't know what to say. She said, "Let's keep this a secret." I nodded my head again. Then she told me to go outside and call my mother. After speaking to the social worker, my mom asked me if I wanted to see her again. I couldn't say a word; I just kept nodding my head, smiling. I was so happy.

When we arrived at home, I went to the dictionary to look

up the word, "lesbian" and after reading what it said I thought, okay, that's what I am. That night I was awake for a long time. When I did sleep, I had a dream of being with that woman. The following day was a Saturday. Everything looked different. I felt that my whole life had changed.

This woman gave me an opportunity to find out about my sexuality and I couldn't turn it down. I was 13 and she was 30 when our affair started. It went on for five years, until I was 18 and she went to live overseas.

The social worker used to make up stories so that I could stay at her house. She used to tell my mother that she was helping me with my studies or taking me to a social work function for kids. My schoolwork improved when I became involved with my social worker. I developed an interest in reading. It began with a school book called *Stories for Work and Play*. The book had stories and poetry in it and I loved it. I began to visit the library and take out other books. Favourites I remember are a book by Carolyn Meyer, *When the Broken Heart Still Beats,* and another book called, *Winter Love*. I don't remember the author. I also read a huge book with a pink cover called *Coming Out*.

My mom always agreed to let me go anywhere with my social worker for any length of time because she trusted her and she trusted me and she could see that I was happy. So I used to sleep over at this woman's place and that is how I learned about sex. The first time I stayed the night with her, she had straight and gay porn magazines on a table in her bedroom. She put me in bed and gave me a story in a magazine to read while she went to have a bath. The story was about a girl driving a van who picked up another girl who was hitchhiking. They became tired and decided to park the van and take a rest in the back. They were facing each other and they started to kiss each other and move their hands over each other's bodies. When my social worker came out of the bath she took the magazine away from me and started to kiss me. Then she started to run her fingers over my vagina and to suck me. She played with my body and I let her do whatever she wanted to do. I tried to be one of the girls in the story and started to touch her and suck her as well. I did everything I remembered from the story. She said she loved me because I was pure and innocent and she kept on telling me, "You are a lesbian. You are a lesbian."

She used to make me breakfast and bring it to me in bed. She would run the bath for me and feel the temperature of the water. She would clean after me and put my clothes out for me. She treated me the way that women treat a child or a husband. In African culture women do all the work. Men sit and watch TV and drink beer unless there is some heavy work.

Once I told her that I loved her and she said, "No, you don't love me. You think you love me because you are still young." I cried because I thought I loved her and she loved me.

I had a friend, a classmate named Siphiwe, who kept proposing to me, telling me he loved me. I was fond of him, so one day when I was 13 or 14, I kissed him. I was rough like a man and I took the initiative. He said, "You are a tomboy!" and pushed me away. I knew I was a tomboy. I knew I was more of a boy than a girl. Siphiwe helped me to decide who I was and we were friends until he died in 2006.

After my experience with Siphiwe, I began to focus all my attention on my relationship with my social worker. When I was 16 she introduced me to some organisations and she took me to a gay and lesbian club at the Carlton Centre and to the Skyline in Hillbrow. I wasn't allowed in because I was too young but my body was well developed so I looked older than I was. Some people suspected that I was under age and they asked questions but she used to say, "This is my kid," and that made them keep quiet.

She didn't kiss me in public. We were partners in the bedroom but in public she was like my tutor or my sister and I used to become very jealous of the older women she was talking to.

When I think of that woman I say, thank you, because she made me see who I was. The girls of nowadays are different. They are always after something, material things. They are not interested in finding out who they are. I was not there when I was 13. I was looking for the truth about myself. I wasn't looking for a way to run away. For me now it feels wrong to have a relationship with a girl who is younger than 18. It is not right for me, but when this woman gave me the opportunity, I decided I could not turn it down. I was experimenting with an older person who could show me the direction.

When I turned 18 I was watching the Felicia Mabuza-Suttle show on TV with my mother one night and they were talking about gays and lesbians. It was just me and my mother in the house. We looked at each other, but I didn't say anything. The next morning I prepared breakfast and I took it to my mother in her room. She said, "What do you want?" I opened the door leading outside because I thought if she was going to hit me I would just run out. I stood near the door with my hand on the door handle and I said, "Do you remember the show we were watching last night?" And she said, "Yes, they were talking about *istabanes*.[1] And I said, "What will you feel if you have a child like that?" And she said, "I know you are like that. I know

---

1 A contemptuous term for gay and lesbian people which can be broadly translated as "hermaphrodite".

that you are *istabane*. I closed the door and said, "What? Why didn't you say anything?" And she said, "I was just waiting for you to tell me."

Then she asked me to sit next to her on the bed and she said, "Each and every family has their child that is disabled. God gave you to me as my disabled child. You are my child. If I throw you out, who is going to take you? I love you like all the other children."

She told me a story about two gay guys she used to work for at the time when she was pregnant with me. One day when she arrived early for work she walked in on them making love. She got such a shock that she immediately put her hand on her stomach and she thought, what will I do if I have a child like this? She said, "By the time I saw that you were like this, I thought about that day and thought that God heard me that day and answered this prayer. And so there is nothing I could do. I had to accept you the way you are."

When I was leaving the room I felt happy and relieved. My mom called me and when I turned around she said, "You don't need to keep any more secrets. If anything happens, come and tell me about it."

My mother told the rest of the family. I didn't come out to anyone. First she told my sisters. They were furious. They said, "This is wrong. We will not accept it." My mother told them "If you are not going to accept her you will have to leave the house with only the things you bought for yourselves. Leave if you want to." She protected me. My sisters saw it was them that had a problem.

My mom paved the way for me to come out. If there was gossip in the community about me she would go and fight for me and I would hear about it afterwards. She was my protector.

She told my relatives about my lifestyle as well, so it was easy for me to go to family gatherings without anybody asking me any questions. My mother did not allow other people to call me *istabane*. She called me that because she didn't know to call me *inkohnkoni*.[2] She didn't know any other language for gay and lesbian people, but she would fight with other people if they called me *istabane*.

After telling my mother, I felt completely free to be myself. I accepted that I was a lesbian and I was not afraid of anyone. I shaved my head and became a tomboy. At weddings and other ceremonies where boys and girls were separated, I would stand on the side of the boys. Once at a wedding, in the same year that I came out to my mother, I was eating with the boys on the boys' side. There are things that boys can eat and girls are not allowed to eat. For example, women are not allowed to eat the head of a cow. I was busy eating with the boys when my cousin noticed me and said, "What is she doing there? She is not supposed to be eating with you guys?" They asked, "What is wrong with him?" So my cousin said, "No, it is not a him, it is a her." I ran for my life.

At school I was a fighter so nobody bullied me. They knew I was a lesbian. I was in standard nine when I came out. I was a runner for the school and I was respected for being a runner. I was not a troublemaker at school. I was quiet and always on time. My uniform was neat and clean and I did my homework. One day I had a fight with a boy in the schoolyard about a girl.

---

2 Literally translated the word means "Blue Wildebeest", an animal found in southern Africa. It is an indigenous, colloquial isiZulu term for lesbians or gay men. It is difficult to find an explanation as to why the Blue Wildebeest should be associated with same-sex sexuality. However, the late Reverend Tsietsi Thandekiso, former minister to a Johannesburg-based black gay and lesbian church, explained that the Wildebeest is sexually indiscriminate, "especially in winter".

The girl approached me and this boy felt threatened. He stared swearing at me, accusing me of turning the girls into lesbians. I was so angry, I stabbed him with my pen. The whole class knew that I had wounded this boy but when the principal came and asked what had happened, nobody accused me. When the boy told the principal it was me who had stabbed him, the principal refused to believe him. "Nkabinde wouldn't do that," he said.

I didn't have any problems in the community like other lesbians. Even when my partners used to come and visit me at home, the boys would show them the way to my house if they said they were going to see *Bee*. This was the name I was given by the soccer coach. He said I moved like a bee on the soccer field. When a bee flies, you can't catch it and when I had the ball no one could catch me. I played third position. I started playing soccer when I was 16. I played for the school and for the Technikon and around the neighbourhood. Soccer was for guys but they allowed me to play if they were short of someone. Then a team was formed in the neighbourhood for girls only and that's when I really made a mark as a soccer player.

The boys respected me and I respected them. I didn't get involved in fights with them. I grew up in a protective community. I could go around with my girlfriends, even at night.

I feel my sexuality was with me from birth. It is not from my ancestors, but my ancestors supported me. When I was a child I didn't have a choice about things like wearing a dress but as I grew up I knew I must express the feelings that were inside me and do what was right for me. My ancestors helped me to become who I was. They guided me knowing that I was going to grow up being the way I am. My sexuality is from childhood.

CHAPTER FOUR

Following the Light

AFTER I FINISHED MATRIC I had some part time jobs as a cashier for the Premier Soccer League and then for Phillips Appliances. I worked over weekends and sometimes during the week. I took some of my savings to pay for my 21st birthday party. My mother wanted to have a big party for me because I was the only child to complete matric, but she was sick so she was not working at the time. I gave my mother some money to buy food for a braai for a few of my friends and I ordered a cake in the shape of a book with, "Happy Birthday, Zandile", written on it in pink icing. I told the man at the bakery to have it ready on 6 December, the Friday before my birthday. When I went to collect the cake the baker gave it to me for no charge. He said, "Take it for your birthday," and he refused to take my money.

It was supposed to be a small party but more and more people kept arriving. My cousin went out to buy more meat so there was plenty of food and the party went on from lunch time till midnight. I felt happy and positive about my future.

I used most of my savings to register for a journalism course at the Pretoria Technikon. I thought this would be a fist step because I love writing and I love telling people's stories. I saw the course advertised in the newspaper. It was a three-year, full-time course and I managed to pay for two years with my part-time jobs and with some friends helping me out with my fees here and there. I stayed with a friend in a flat in Pretoria and came back to Meadowlands over weekends and in the holidays.

I thought I would find a way to finish my journalism course and become a writer but my ancestors had other plans for me.

In February 1998 my mother was admitted to the Helen Joseph Hospital. She had a headache that wouldn't go away. Nobody knew the cause of the headache. The doctors didn't tell us. When I went to visit my mother at the hospital, I had an experience that was so strange that even today it makes me feel dizzy when I remember it.

My mother asked me to go with her to the bathroom. She was weak and I put my arm around her to help her walk, but even though she was not well she was making conversation, asking me about my life and the girls I was dating. In the bathroom, my mother stood in front of the basin facing the mirror. I looked over her head because I was taller than her. I saw my own reflection in the mirror but not my mother's reflection. I looked away and then looked back at the mirror, thinking something was wrong with my eyes. Again I saw my own reflection but not my mother's. It was as if my mother was not present, as if she didn't exist. I was shocked by what had happened but I didn't say anything. I took my mom back to her bed and after making sure she was comfortable, my sister and I went home. We thought she was getting better because she was calm when we left.

On our way home I heard somebody telling me that my mother was going to be taken away. I turned to my sister, thinking she was the one talking to me, "What did you say?" I asked. "Nothing," she said.

I went back to my grandfather's place. I had my own room

in the backyard at that time. During the night, I heard more voices. I thought maybe I was losing my mind because there was nobody around except me. I went to buy a beer, thinking it would help me to sleep. It didn't help. The voices were still there. First they were talking, then they were shouting so loudly that it felt as if someone was hitting me on the head with a hammer. I was sweating and my head was pounding as if I had a fever. Something strange was happening to me and there was nobody to help me understand.

After a sleepless night, I was so exhausted I had no strength left to resist so I started paying attention and trying to hear what the voices were saying. They warned that they were going to take my mother away. I asked, "Where are you taking her?" I was told I would know the answer soon. It was very early in the morning. There was a little light in the room. I looked around, squinting to see if there was anybody there, the owners of the voices. There was nobody. I asked, "Why are you taking my mother away?" I waited for an answer that made sense to me. The answer came: "She was called to do the work of her ancestors but she refused." I heard the words but still I didn't understand that the voices were the voices of my ancestors calling for somebody from their clan to carry on their work in the world.

I waited till six am to call my sister. "Come with me to the hospital," I said. Thuli was still half asleep but she could hear that I was stressed and she agreed to meet me in an hour's time. I didn't tell her I was hearing voices because I thought she would say I was crazy or accuse me of being drunk.

My sister's fiancé, Patrick, drove us to the hospital. I jumped out of the car and ran to my mother's bed in Ward 13. I found her in a worse condition than before. She was asleep in a bed like a child's cot and there were intravenous tubes going into both her arms. I woke her up and tried to speak to her but she couldn't focus her eyes and she didn't seem to hear me. She looked around the room, avoiding me. It was difficult for her to breathe. She whispered when she spoke. She asked where my brothers and sisters were and then she asked about the white necklace she gave me for my 18th birthday. I told her it was at home. "Wear it," she said, "You must wear it." At that moment the voices came back, speaking in a chorus inside my head, telling me they were taking my mother away.

I ran out of the room to find the doctor, leaving Thuli and Patrick at my mother's bedside. Finally, I found him. I was upset and I demanded to know what was happening with mother. "What is causing the headaches? When can we take her home?" The doctor didn't answer my questions. He said my mother could not be healed.

Patrick suggested we consult a prophet. Normally in my culture, if a person is sick, we seek help from western medicine and traditional medicine. We drove to the house of a prophet. Patrick knew this man. When we arrived there, he immediately said: "You have come because of a sick woman. This woman is crying for her children. There is nothing I can do." He leant forward and tapped me on the shoulder and looking in my eyes he said, "You know. *You* know. You *know*…"

I grew up in a family that believes in prophets and sangomas and I knew that some were true and others were charlatans. I decided I didn't believe this man so I didn't pay attention to what he said.

It was raining when we left the prophet's house. We went back to the hospital. At three in the afternoon we were walking along the passage to my mother's ward. I saw my aunts and uncles standing at the door. They were crying. As I approached them, the voices came back. This time they were saying that my mother had been taken away. I ran inside and found a nurse standing beside my mother's bed. The nurse said my mother had passed away five minutes ago. My mother looked as if she was asleep. Even in death, she was such a pretty woman with her delicate feminine features. She looked peaceful with her hands folded across her chest. I leaned forward and kissed her. "I love you, mom," I said. I was too late. She couldn't hear me.

My sister and my aunts started gathering my mother's clothes and washing things together. I thought about my father. How would we find him to tell him that my mother had died? He was living somewhere, but where? Nobody knew. He had disappeared from our lives and not even my grandfather had an idea where to find him. I took my mother's hand and removed her wedding ring. My mom had never taken the ring off, not even after the divorce.

* * *

When we arrived at the house, some family members were waiting for us. In traditional culture when somebody passes away that person's bed is taken out of the room and the mattress is placed on the floor. After this, all the mirrors in the house are covered with blankets. Everything is done silently. No music is allowed. My aunt and uncle removed the bed and covered the mirrors.

I didn't cry. I helped my mother's youngest sister, Ntombi, and my uncles to move the furniture and prepare for the funeral. Later, my Aunt Zodwa arrived. She took my mom's clothes out of her wardrobe and folded them neatly in a bag.

When my grandfather – my father's father – came, everyone could feel the tension between the two families. Much later, at around nine or ten at night, my father arrived with his sister, my aunt. Somebody must have found him and told him about my mother's death. When I looked at him I could see that he came with war; he came to fight. He walked into the house like a dictator, telling us what to do. He told us it was his wife who had passed away and he was going to bury her. A fight broke out between my father and my sisters. My father had divorced my mother and nobody knew where he was living. What right did he have to tell us how to bury our mother? The atmosphere was so tense. It reminded me of the fighting in the house when I was a young child.

I took my cigarettes and went and sat outside on the pavement. I was asking myself, which rules allowed my father to behave like this? When my father walked out of the house with my aunt running after him, his face was black with anger. He looked at me and I looked at him but we didn't say anything. I went inside and found my sisters were full of emotion.

* * *

Preparations for the funeral went on through the week. Neighbours came bringing their donations of money and biscuits and prayers. Outside it was raining and inside the house was full of sorrow and tears.

My aunt dictated a letter to my mother's great uncle. I wrote it in English and had to rewrite it in Zulu after my aunt told me the relative didn't speak any English. I remember this incident because in spite of our grief, my aunt and I laughed when we realized what I had done.

We waited for my uncle Vusumuzi from Empangeni to arrive. He sent instructions for my sisters to find a cow and a goat and when he arrived, he slaughtered the goat in the yard of the house. A goat is slaughtered to open up the way for the deceased and to combine the spirit of the deceased with the spirits of the ancestors who have already passed away. The men in the family do the slaughtering and the women cook the meat in big pots. Only the family members eat the goat and it all has to be finished in one day. Even the bones of the goat are burned because nothing must remain.

The women stayed at home while my uncle Vusumuzi and other men in the family went to check the grave and speak to the ancestors there. I felt completely alone. The voices had stopped by this time and I didn't think of anything because my emotions were so strong. I felt that I was lost. Without my mother, I didn't know where I belonged.

Throughout the week, I was lifting pots and doing the men's work in the house and I wore a sports cap and a man's overalls. I could see that one of my great aunts, my mother's aunt, was not happy about this. She called me aside and said I must wear a skirt and a doek on my head because this is what our tradition expects. I argued with her. I told her I knew how to respect my mother in my heart and my mother didn't know me wearing a skirt. She would not give up and she went and talked to my aunt Zodwa, hoping my aunt would force me to wear a skirt, but Zodwa agreed with me. She said, "Her mother passed away knowing that this child was wearing pants. Please don't confuse the spirit of her mother because when the spirit of her mother comes around looking for her children and she doesn't see that child, what will you say? So just let the child wear her pants. That is who she is."

On Friday the hearse arrived with my mother's corpse in it at the same time as a truck arrived with the cow. My uncle went to the hearse and as the coffin was being carried into the house he spoke to the ancestors, explaining what was happening and asking the ancestors to open the doors for my mother. The coffin was brought into the house and placed on a grass mat in my mom's bedroom near the window, facing where the sun rises. Three white candles were burned for the ancestors to bring the bright spirit.

That night, the coffin was opened so that we could see my mother's face. The elders and my oldest sister sat next to the coffin while each one of us children went up to say goodbye to my mom. Afterwards I went outside and sat on the pavement, smoking. I watched the lights going out in my street until it was very late and I was sitting in darkness.

On Saturday morning people from the Zionist Church and neighbours came to a service in the yard of the house and in the afternoon the hearse took my mother's coffin to the Dobsonville cemetery. My uncle walked in front of the coffin, talking to the ancestors, explaining why we were taking my mother out of her house and to the grave. My mom was a member of a burial society. The women from the society were dressed in royal blue and powder blue uniforms. They formed two lines and sang hymns to my mother while her coffin passed by.

The grass mat and the blankets from my mother's room were cut into pieces and put in the grave with the coffin. As I went forward to throw soil onto my mom's coffin, I felt so empty inside that I cried. It was the first time I had cried since she passed away.

People said my father was at the cemetery but I didn't see him there. He came to the house after the funeral but I didn't speak to him.

Ten days later the priest came to do the cleansing and free our spirits. For the next three months of official mourning, my great aunt stayed on to assist us. We all wore mourning bands. My sisters and the other women covered their heads with doeks. I shaved my head like my brothers and the men in the family.

* * *

After we had done all these things, I wanted to go back to complete my journalism course at the Pretoria Tech, but I didn't have enough money to pay the fees. I tried to find my father to ask him to help me but he was nowhere to be found. I was unsettled and because of the financial difficulties, I couldn't give my studies my full attention. I went to Pretoria and stayed for a couple of months with my friends and then returned to Soweto for a while before returning to Pretoria to complete my course.

On my way to Pretoria the second time, I heard the voices again. This time they were telling me to go to a river. I tried to ignore them but they were so loud and insistent that I lost track of where I was and the next thing I knew I was inside an ambulance and a paramedic was leaning over me and asking my name.

I was admitted to Kalafong hospital and discharged after being examined. I left the hospital and took a taxi. I thought I was on my way back to the Technikon but discovered that I was on my way to Johannesburg. Again the voices were telling me to go to a river. Which river? How? I tried to ignore them but the more I tried, the louder they became. My head was spinning and I was so hot I felt I was on fire. Then suddenly everything was dark and I couldn't see a thing. I heard the sound of drums and whistling and people talking. The noise was so loud that I thought my head was going to burst. When the taxi arrived in Johannesburg, I immediately took a meter taxi to Soweto. I collapsed in the back seat and when I arrived at my parents' house, I went straight to the bedroom and fell onto the bed. I was exhausted from the fighting that was going on inside me.

I don't know who took me to the Sterkfontein mental institution and I don't know how long I had been there when I became conscious that I was not in my room at home. The nurses told me my sisters had brought me there. After some days I began to feel calmer and the noise in my head was not so overwhelming but just when I was about to be discharged, it started again. I cried and screamed with frustration.

The nurses injected me to make me sleep but every morning at three am I would wake up. This is the time to communicate with the ancestors. They were waking me up to communicate but I didn't understand at that time. One day when the ancestors woke me up in the early hours of the morning, I lay on my bed in the hospital feeling that I could not go on any longer because I didn't understand and I felt desperate. Suddenly I saw a light coming through a window as if someone was pointing a powerful torch directly in my face. I don't know where the light was coming from. There was nobody there. I heard a voice telling me to follow. It was as if somebody or something was moving my body without my will. I stood up and followed. Normally the gates were locked but that morning I found them open and for once there was no security guard at the gate.

I walked out into the night with nobody to stop me. The voices were singing in a chorus, encouraging me to keep on going. I walked and walked without knowing my destination. I walked until I lost consciousness.

When I came around I was lying on the floor in a strange room and I could not remember anything about my life. I didn't know who I was or where I came from. It was as if the past had vanished. I lay on the floor feeling anxious and confused, trying to get my bearings. I felt so lonely and sad. I must have fallen asleep because the next thing I remember is the light seeping around the corners of the curtains. Everything in the room looked hazy and unclear. I threw aside the blanket that was covering me and tried to stand up. My body was heavy and sluggish, as if I had been drugged. It took all my strength to get myself onto my feet. I walked across the room with slow, heavy steps. There was a mirror on the wall. My gray complexion and the black rings under my eyes made me look like a woman more than three times my age. My hand was shaking as I held it up to my cheek. I didn't recognise myself. I turned away from the mirror and looked around this strange room that I had never seen before and I was filled with fear.

Then I heard a scratching sound that became more and more violent. The skin on my head was prickling and the blood pounded in my ears. I forced my heavy body towards the door and pulled it open. At first I could see nothing there except a long, empty passage but the next moment, the whole building seemed to reverberate with a thumping noise as though somebody or something was being flung against the wall. I saw a creature that seemed to be both human and animal. I prayed for help as it moved towards me and then I lost consciousness.

Later, I found myself in a place that looked like a church. A man was there with me. He looked like a priest or a deacon. He gave me a change of clothes and invited me to a meal. Afterwards he took me into an empty room and left me there. Again there were voices, this time telling me that I should leave this place. I found myself running along unfamiliar, dark roads. I ran until I reached a shelter like a cave under a bridge. I hid there until morning.

Eventually, after many visions and voices, which took me into strange places that I had never seen before, I arrived in the street outside my parents' house. I was guided by the bright light and a voice I recognised, although I couldn't give it a name or a face.

My brother, Sifiso, found me wandering in the street outside the house on the day of my sister's wedding. She had a traditional wedding and some of the aunts were at the house from my mother's side. They asked me where I had been. I couldn't tell them. They saw there was something wrong with me so they took me to a sangoma.

The sangoma was a man. As soon as I saw the skins of a snake and a monkey outside his consulting room, I began to scream and refused to go inside. My sister and my brother-in-law bought some herbs from him and when we arrived home they burned them to calm me and put me to sleep. I was so exhausted I fell into a deep sleep. I dreamed of a house that was like a church. All the walls of the building were white and it felt peaceful and welcoming. A woman appeared and I heard a voice telling me that this is where I must go to answer the call.

My aunt offered to look after me at her house but I was so disturbed that it was difficult for her to even take me in the car. I fought and screamed because of the continual noise in my head of drums beating and people talking loudly all at the same time. My family was so concerned that they took me to another sangoma, a woman this time. When I saw her, I calmed down. I recognised her from somewhere and I found her presence comforting. She said, "You are in the right place now. You have to stop being stubborn to answer your calling." When I explained about the voices and what was happening with me, she didn't say that I had to go back to Sterkfontein and she didn't look at me as if I was mad. I felt that she understood me. I knew that she was the woman from my dream who would show me the way.

Before being accepted for training, I went to stay with my aunt for a month. The voices continued to speak to me day and night. My aunt tried to help me in her way. She called some of her congregation from the Church of Zion to pray in the house and she asked the priest to perform a cleansing ceremony. I fought with the man. People say I was powerful like a tiger and I didn't want anyone to touch me.

A few days later I had a vision of a snake wrapping itself around my body and speaking to me, saying, "Don't be afraid. I just want you to go and answer the calling. Go and do what you have to do."

* * *

On a Saturday in May, my sisters took me to my trainer's house to begin my training as a sangoma. My sisters had told my trainer that I was a lesbian and she said I would be healed and get married to a man. I didn't know about this when I began my training.

After a small ceremony, I was told to get undressed and soak in a bath of cold water, filled with herbs before being dressed in red traditional cloth. I was taken to a room where other trainees and practicing sangomas were waiting for me. I sat on a grass mat and some herbs were burned between my legs. My body was covered with two white sheets.

I heard the sound of the drums beating and felt the rhythm in my body. Suddenly the snake that I saw at my aunt's house appeared between my legs and wrapped itself around me. They say that a powerful man's voice exploded out of my mouth. It was the voice of my ancestor Nkunzi saying that he had come to claim his bag of bones. From this moment, I took my ancestor's name as my own.

CHAPTER FIVE

Remembering the Ancient Paths

THE NAME NKUNZI MEANS "black bull." Nobody is exactly sure why my great uncle was given this name. Some members of the family say his father gave him the name because of his pitch-black complexion; others say it was because of his reputation for fighting with the boys in the village, usually over girls.

I Nkunzi Emnyama Iyazona Izithole
(The Black Bull ravishes the heifers)

Akukho ntombi eyahlula Isoka lase Mangwaneni
(There is no maiden that overcomes the courting youth of Mangwaneni)

Musa ndoda uku valela i Nkunzi esibayeni nezi nkomazi
(Do not, man, close the bull in the kraal with the cows)

Ngoba ngakusasa u yakuzithola zonke zimithi
(Because tomorrow you will find them all pregnant)

Nenzani Bafana nibamba iNkunzi emsileni
(What are you doing boys, holding onto the bull by its tail)

Nazimbela ingodi emini libalele
(You dig yourselves a grave in daylight)

Awubo ngiya we Nkunzi Emnyama ungiye uze uqethuke
(I advance, Black Bull, you advance on me and you fail)

There were many sides to Nkunzi. He was a Zulu man, a dictator who made the rules and expected people to obey; he liked to drink traditional beer and expected his wives to serve him; he was a fighter who could be abusive and even violent at times; and he liked the company of women. He was also a dreamer who would withdraw from human company and spend hours, sometimes days, in silence. He knew the land and he had respect for the seasons and the cycles of nature. He knew the names of plants and herbs and what they could be used for, and he could predict the weather. He could tell when the time was right to plant and to harvest his crops because of the position of the stars. He lived in harmony with nature.

Nkunzi was 45 when he died. One day before he passed away, he was sitting alone on a favourite rock overlooking the valley when a woman from the family went to find him. He told her, "After I die, one of the grandchildren will take my name and follow after me, doing things in a different way." It was the first time he had spoken about his death and the family knew that the end of his life was not far away. Nobody had a clue which grandchild would be called to follow in his footsteps and what he meant by doing things "in a different way."

* * *

During my training I had to be purified so that there was nothing blocking me from hearing my ancestors and becoming a healer. A sangoma's training is about finding balance so that we can live with respect for all life. In the training we find our place in relationship with God, our ancestors and our family. We also learn how to work with the elements of air, water, fire and earth and with the four directions: north, south, west and east. Usually when somebody begins their training they are given red traditional cloth to wear. Red is the colour of fire and transformation. The dancing to the beat of drums in sangoma ceremonies prepares us to welcome our ancestors. It connects us with our bodies and with the earth.

In African culture, the community is especially important. In my community I learn about who is higher and who has gone deeper down, and I learn about who I am and who I am not. When I became a trainee sangoma, I became part of a community of sangomas – elders and trainees – who supported me and assisted me while I learned how to live the life of a sangoma. I stayed with my trainer and my sangoma community for eight months.

In the first month I was taught how to recognise my ancestors. My trainer told me that if I see a sign, like a snake, I should not be afraid but see it as a symbol for my ancestors and know that they are communicating with me. If I feel a breath or a breeze running up the back of my neck, I should know that this is my ancestor telling me he or she is present. The more I learned about the signs, the more I began to feel my ancestors around me and in me. After being trained, when I saw a sign or felt something on the back of my neck, I could say with confidence, "They are here."

Our ancestors use different parts of our bodies to make us listen to them. Mainly with me it is the back of my body. I will feel something up my spine and when I relax, they will begin to talk to me. Or sometimes I will just hear someone talking. If I didn't know it was one of my ancestors, I would look around to see who was there but, now that I know, I will keep quiet and listen to what my ancestor wants to say to me.

Next I had to learn how to control my ancestors. If you can't control your ancestors, they can destroy your body. In the beginning, before I understood how to work with my ancestors, I used to roar like a lion when I felt something moving up my spine and gripping the back of my neck. Sometimes, one side of my body would feel as if it was dying and I would become paralysed as if I had a stroke. I used to panic and think, if he kills this half of my body, I won't be able to do anything. After my trainer taught me how to respond, I would talk to Nkunzi and say, "Don't disturb me. Talk to me. I am listening," and when he was calm I would say, "Okay. I am listening. I can feel you are here. What do you want?"

Nkunzi is a fighter. When he first appeared, he was fighting. He will fight with me inside my own body until I say, "Okay, what do you want?" In my training, I had to learn to dance sitting down with my legs crossed so that I could control the spirit of Nkunzi in me. I wanted to stand up and dance but I wasn't allowed to. My trainer said, "No. This is not the time for you to stand up. You have to sit. The time for you to stand will arrive." So I had to struggle with the spirit of Nkunzi and learn to keep him under control and this went on for nearly two months of the training and I am still learning. The first stage is when my ancestor came out. It is called *ukushyela*. This is when I had to learn how to dance while seated. The stage of dancing while standing up is called *ukusuma*.

My trainer taught me how to be on guard because the ancestors will come in their own time and if I am not prepared,

I might jump up with surprise while walking down the street and be hit by a car. I also had to learn how to obey. I was stubborn and I didn't know how to obey when I began my training.

I was taught how to throw the bones. When a sangoma throws the bones for a client he or she can see the whole of that person's environment, from the most intimate details to the society at large and even the whole world. The bones will show every person and every situation that is having an effect on the client. Although I had no experience of throwing the bones, I understood quickly and I could easily point out the signs for a car or a married couple or a person who had been involved in an accident. I was so quick that my trainer said, "Your ancestors are fast. You will not spend much time here."

I also learned how to work with my ancestors to find the herbs I need. Sometimes when the ancestors come, they will just give me a herb the way it is and tell me that this is for a stroke, this is for heartburn, and this is for someone who is paralysed. At other times I have to go and find the herbs I am looking for. I have an idea of what I need but I don't know where it is. I go to Bushbuckridge to collect herbs.[1] Before going there I must fast and abstain from sex so that I am pure.

Some trees are dangerous and can be used for their negative powers; others are guarded by dangerous snakes. I learned that I must collect herbs when I am in my ancestral spirit rather than my own spirit so that I am protected and if a snake attacks me I am on the alert and can kill the snake before it strikes me. I have never had a bad experience with snakes. The only time I encountered a snake while gathering herbs was when a baby

---

1 Bushbuckridge is in the Limpopo province. It is known for its indigenous trees and plants and for its many sangomas/traditional healers. The barks, roots, bulbs, seeds and fruit are used for traditional medicines.

snake managed to get into my sack. When I opened my sack I saw the snake there.

I understood the herbs quickly. I had a knowledge that was from my ancestors that was working in me. I was very lucky because I found the herb that is used for creating lightning. When it is in the tree, this herb is sticky like jam and it is so dark in colour that you will think it is part of the tree that has been burnt by fire. But when you touch it, it is soft. If you mix it with other herbs you can make lightning with it. My trainer told me, "You are very lucky. Your ancestors are with you. But be careful who you tell about this because another sangoma will kill you for this herb."

One of the male sangomas who accompanied me was poisoned because he found a lucky stone and another sangoma was jealous. The jealous sangoma told him to touch the branch of a tree that is poisonous and because he didn't know and he didn't suspect the other sangoma, he touched the tree and the liquid from that tree, which was still fresh, went into his eyes and onto his body. Within a few hours he was dead.

I was fascinated by the herbs and what Nkunzi and my other ancestors were teaching me. I was open and I lapped up everything that I was told. There was so much to learn and this was just the beginning. I learned to recognise the plants and my ancestors told me what to use them for. I also learned the side affects and consequences of some of the plants, like *Skanama*, for example. Skanama is the reddish bark of a tree. It is ground up very fine. When the leaves of the tree are still wet, Skanama looks like beetroot and if you touch it without gloves you start to itch. The first time my trainer gave me this herb to grind, I took it and started to grind it without gloves. My whole body began to itch. When I told my trainer, she laughed at me and said, "Now you know what skanama does!"

I learned about *Umkhanyakude*, which means, "you are bright from far away". It is a yellowish and greenish coloured tree with thorns all around it. It looks as if it is still growing into green. I was shown how to peel the side of the trunk of the tree and to dig out its roots. It can be used for people who have to deal with the law, like court cases, and it can also be used for beauty. If you bath in Umkhanyakude and mix it with other herbs before you go to court, the judge will look at you and feel that you are pure and he will feel pity for you. He won't see the crime you have committed because of the brightness that is in you.

Luru is white in colour. It comes from the branches of a tree. It has to be peeled and dried and made into small sticks like match sticks. If it is added to a man's bath with other herbs, it makes him attractive to women.

The cure for STIs comes from the roots of a tree that is known as *Labatheka*. It is a big tree that has a strong smell. It smells like mint. It is hard work to get the roots of the tree using a pick. The roots are a dark brownish colour and after they have been ground they become brownish and whitish. The ground powder is mixed with other herbs and boiled. A person with STIs drinks the mixture for four days.

* * *

After I could dance on my feet without losing control, I had to learn to find objects that were hidden. To prepare for the test, I was told to clean the house and the grounds so that I became familiar with the place and could introduce my ancestors to every corner of my trainer's property. I learned how to control my mind and to communicate with my ancestors so that they could guide me by sounds or signs to the hidden object. My trainer would hide things like some of my beads and I had to tell her what was hidden and then to find it.

Normally a trainee sangoma's family will hide things when they come to visit, to prove that the trainee has the spirit of the ancestor with them. My family took pity on me and they didn't hide very much while I was still in training.

The next stage of the training is when you learn to work with your ancestors to take out their stubbornness. It is known as *khalela inkani*.[2] Many sangomas run away in this stage because it is so difficult. You get in touch with some of the deeper secrets of being a sangoma. You work with the inner soul of the ancestors. You do this work for your clan, for all your ancestors.

If your ancestor was abusive, that abusiveness must be taken out. I had to deal directly with my ancestral spirits and whatever had to be cleansed and purified in my ancestors had to be cleansed and purified in my own body. My body was used to fight out my ancestors' stubbornness. Each day when I danced I was dealing with a characteristic of an ancestor that had to be removed so that it didn't get in the way of healing. Even if somebody has an ancestor who was a killer, that killer instinct must be taken out so that the ancestor can become a healer.

In this stage of *khalela inkani*, I couldn't look into the eyes of a white person. My trainer used to take me into town in handcuffs to tame my ancestor's spirit in me. People would stare at me but she just ignored them. She took me to an office where some white men she knew were working. I roared like a lion. I wanted to attack the men. All the time my trainer was talking to my ancestor, telling him, "These people are like you. You must

---

2   Literally, "to cry for stubbornness"

learn to sit with these people." And she would say to me, "Your ancestor is so stubborn. If he is fighting with white people, how will you survive? One day you will have a white man in your consulting room, are you going to kill that man?" She forced me to look into the eyes of one of these men. I finally managed and when I looked into his eyes I took his powers and after that I became calm and my ancestor started to understand.

Nkunzi was a stubborn Zulu man, the kind of dictator that says, "I won't listen to a woman. A man's word is final." He was like that. So he had to learn to listen to others. In that process I also had to learn to listen to others because I was not used to listening to others either. Nkunzi is my dominant ancestor. In the beginning, he was not prepared to make room for other ancestors to come in. He had to learn to accept that other ancestors would also make use of my body. His attitude was, "This is my body. I found it. I built it. No one is supposed to be there but me. I am the only one that is supposed to be in this body."

Sangomas work with different kinds of ancestors: ancestors who share the same bloodline; ancestors from the village and the nation; ancestors that come from other parts of the world; and ancestors that are part of everything that exists. In the time of *khalela inkani*, Nkunzi had to be taught to allow other ancestors in so that if I am out in the street and I meet another ancestral spirit who wants to work through me, Nkunzi will not start to fight with this spirit inside my body because the fighting could destroy me.

Some of the trainees who were with me in the beginning left before the end of the training and one even passed away because she was so stubborn. There were 14 of us who stayed right up to graduation.

The preparation for the initiation ceremony is demanding. For four days we only drink water and have one bowl of soft porridge in the morning. On the fifth day there is no food. The night before the ceremony, cuts are made in our flesh and a mixture of herbs is placed in the wounds. This helps us to become more sensitive and prepares us to welcome our ancestors.

Each trainee's family buys a goat for the initiation ceremony. The goat is hidden and we have to find it. After the goat has been found and slaughtered, the *inyongo*[3] is hidden and we have to find that. This is an important part of initiation. The night before the ceremony, we prayed for our ancestors to help us. I dreamed of an old man with a pigeon on his shoulder. He was looking at me and tapping his pocket. I looked at him, thinking he was going to say something but he didn't say a word. When I woke up in the morning, I told my trainer the dream and she told me, "Your *inyongo* is in a pocket but which pocket you do not know."

The following night we started dancing while sitting down, calling our ancestors to be with us. I had found my goat and the time came in the ceremony for it to be slaughtered and for me to drink the blood of the goat. This is a very big step and many don't succeed. My trainer said, "Are you ready?" I said "Yes," and I opened my mouth, with my head turned upwards to catch the blood of the goat at the moment that it was slaughtered. If you vomit that blood, they say you don't have the ancestor spirit in you. With me, I became so thirsty I just grabbed it. I drank more than others and I didn't vomit.

After this, those trainees who have drunk the blood of the goat begin to dance and while dancing we have to look for our *inyongos*. There was a huge crowd present, including my family and all the families of all the initiates. My trainer was standing

---

3 The gall bladder of a goat

far away in a corner. She was praying there. She told people, "If Nkunzi finds it, come and tell me." As I was dancing, the white pigeon from my dream appeared. I followed it. First it settled next to an old sangoma and I went up to her but my *inyongo* was not with her. I followed the bird to an old man, who was sitting next to the verandah of the house. He was wearing a T-shirt with a pocket. I leaned over and took my *inyongo* out of his pocket. As I did this, I heard somebody shouting, "Nkunzi's got it!"

My trainer ran towards me, shouting, "Don't touch her! "Don't touch her!" She knew that if anybody touched me at that moment, the spirit of Nkunzi in me would begin to fight. I gave the *inyongo* to my trainer and she braided it into my hair. The next challenge was to find the bone from the knee joint of the goat. This *ithambo* is made into a bracelet, which we wear whenever we take part in a sangoma ceremony. It was easy for me to find the *ithambo* because the bird settled on the bonnet of my brother's car and when I opened it, the bone was there. I gave it to my trainer and she tied it to my wrist.

The most difficult stage of the initiation happens in water – a river or a dam – in the darkest hours of the night. I was taken to the Klipspruit dam. My two sisters and a few of the elders were present. Family members must accompany the initiate on this part of the journey in case of drowning. Many don't survive.

My trainer asked me, "Do you still remember the *Inknyamba*[4] that you saw when you first came to me?" I nodded. She said, "You might meet him again inside the water. Be ready and be careful."

The ancestors of white people live in the river. If I could have an ancestor of a white person, I would be rich and I would be blessed because they are more powerful than anyone. I can

---

4 Powerful one

create fire and lightning if I have white ancestors. Their power is unique. If I am in the river and I have the spirit of a white person, I can mix something from the river and from the air; I can mix oil and water and make one thing. The ancestors of the water help the ancestors of the earth to see under water.

I threw a sacrificial offering into the river and walked into the water. As soon as I was under the water I saw green eyes staring back at me. I jumped out of the water. I was so afraid. My trainer was shouting at me, "Go back! Go back!" My body was trembling. "I can't! I can't," I cried. "Don't be stubborn! Go back!" My trainer jumped into the water with me and pushed my head under the water with all her strength. I could feel that I was standing on top of the *Inknyamba*. My trainer was outside the water by this time. She was holding my traditional cloth in the water and I heard her saying, "Nkunzi, she is going away. Please try to find her."

The first time I was under the water I was in my normal spirit, I wasn't in my ancestral spirit. This is why I came out of the water immediately and I was afraid. The second time, my trainer told me to call my ancestors and she called to Nkunzi to come out. When my ancestors came I wasn't afraid anymore.

The *Inknyamba* was taking me down the river. My trainer asked some of the elders to bring me back so they got into the water and brought me back to the side of the river. Then they climbed out and left me there. The *Inknyamba* started to make a circle under the water and my trainer shouted: "Go deeper in the place of the circle and take what is yours!" So I went down, down, down to the deepest part of the river, where the *Inknyamba* was leading me, and grabbed my bag of bones. As it did this, I began to lose my strength and I became powerless. The *Inknyamba* pulled me to the surface of the water and disappeared. My trainer was waiting for me. She pulled me out of the river and wrapped my traditional cloth around me. My sister told me she was crying.

We went back to my trainer's house to dancing and the sound of drums beating. I had to find my ring. This was the final challenge. I noticed some elderly sangomas seated on one side. One of them had an *ukhamba*[5] with medicine in it and as we were dancing I heard someone telling me to put my hand in that *ukhamba*. As I did this, the women began to ululate. My trainer asked, "Who got it?" They all shouted, "Nkunzi got it!" Again she cried out, "Don't touch her." She came and tied the ring in the front of my hair. I was so proud. Finally, I was a qualified sangoma.

A feast had been prepared for all the new sangomas with every kind of food that we dreamed of when we were fasting, and to show that we were now qualified, nobody was allowed to talk to us without taking out some money.

All the initiates were asked to pick a song. I chose a song about going home:

Ekhaya bayangimemeza
(Come home, they are calling me)

Bathi mangibuye
(They say I should come back)

Ngoba sengiqedile umsebenzi
(Because I have finished the job)

---

5 Calabash

Ngisitholile isikhwama sikamkhulu
(I have found my grandfather's bag)

A week after my 24th birthday I returned home holding the wooden healer's stick belonging to my McKenzie clan grandmother. The red and white beads I was wearing came to me first in a dream and I have worn them ever since. The white beads are for power and the red beads are for the fire in me. The black and white beads together represent the ancestors from the water. I had been to fetch my ancestors and my life would never be the same again.

When I returned home, I did not have my original face because I had Nkunzi's spirit in me and I had lost a lot of weight because my body was not yet used to having the ancestors working inside me. Friends and neighbours came to congratulate me and there was dancing and celebrations. My father was the only one from my family who was not happy. He was full of anger because my guiding ancestor was from my mother's side of the family and not from the Nkabinde side.

A goat and chickens were slaughtered and some of my blood was combined with the blood of the goat and smeared on a tree outside the house and on a post inside the house as a sign to the ancestors that they are welcome.

I thanked my trainer in the traditional way by putting a blanket around her shoulders while she was dancing, and I took the herbs that I would need for my practice and my bag of bones into my new consulting room that my family had built for me. My trainer gave my sisters and me the *imyalo*.[6] She told me that my consulting room is for healing and I must never have sex with

---

6   Rules for living the life of a sangoma

anyone there. I was warned that other sangomas might tempt me to break the rules because of jealousy.

My trainer instructed an elderly sangoma to stay and watch over me for a week. She had to teach my youngest brother, Linda, to beat the drum for me and to communicate with my ancestor who might take over my body unexpectedly during the night.

CHAPTER SIX

Finding the Balance

I WAS STILL A LESBIAN after I completed my initiation as a sangoma. My trainer told my family, "There is nothing we can do."

When my memory started coming back, my trainer made me bathe in herbs she had prepared and she asked me over and over again if my feelings had changed. I told her my feelings towards women were stronger than ever. I would look at a woman getting dressed and find myself wanting her, wanting to hold her. I couldn't express my feelings because I was still in training and the women were my elders but I was attracted to them. If Nkunzi did not want me to be a lesbian I don't believe I would have had these feelings. He would have given me a male partner and I would have been happy with that. Nkunzi accepts me as a lesbian. He understands my feelings. Nkunzi knew he was going to use my body long before I did.

One night during my training I dreamed I was sleeping with a girl, making love to her. When I looked at myself in the dream I saw that I had male genitals and when I looked at the girl, I saw that she had the face of my trainer. I woke up in a sweat and discovered that the bottom half of my body was wet. I stayed in an outside room in the yard. I covered myself and ran to my trainer's house. I needed to speak to her immediately about my dream.

She was awake and when I opened the door of her bedroom she was sitting up in bed. She was naked. She looked at me with surprise and although I was used to seeing her breasts at any time of the day, she quickly covered herself and asked, "What's wrong?" I asked her the same question, "What's wrong with you?" And she said, "I had a terrible dream." And I said, "Me too. I had a terrible dream."

She got out of bed and covered her body. We went inside the lounge and we were sitting opposite one another there and she said, "Tell me your dream." And I told her, "I dreamed that this lower part of my body was male and I was having sex with you." My trainer shook her head and I said, "What's wrong?" And she said, "I had the same dream. That is why I have woken up. Your ancestor wants to sleep with me."

She sat down with me that night and warned me. "Be careful, my child, because if your ancestor loved a lot of women, you will end up doing wrong things. You had better control him. Don't let him control you when it comes to women. You must learn to control him."

From that day onwards, my trainer never walked naked in front of me again. She would always cover herself. She acted as if I was Nkunzi and she had to be careful not to encourage me.

Nkunzi loves women, especially young women. If I am with a woman of 21 or 22, normally Nkunzi will want to have sex with her. I will feel his presence as if someone is touching my shoulders and sometimes I see the legs and genitals of a man. This is one way he shows himself to me. I have more power when Nkunzi is in me, especially when we both desire the same woman. When this happens, I change. I become so strong. He takes control of my body and even the sounds I make are different. The woman I am with will tell me, "Your eyes are changing." Women I have slept with say my eyes become red or green and I become so wild and strong. Women tell me my body becomes very heavy and when I come my partner will say, "In that moment you were not yourself. What was happening?" I will make a sound like a lion roaring. That is how I know that Nkunzi is satisfied.

After sex I will hear someone saying, "Light a candle." That is how I know Nkunzi has got what he wants. I never question him. I just get up immediately and light a candle, and then I go to sleep and leave the candle burning until morning. I am not sure why he wants a candle. I never question why. I think maybe I am opening up the way for him.

I have slept with gay women and straight women, married women and single women. I love the challenge of straight women, especially if they are married or have partners. I always say, "If you experience the touch of a woman you will never want a man again." Nkunzi doesn't have a problem with my sex life but if he is not happy with my choice of a woman, I will end up fighting a lot with that woman and eventually I don't even feel sexually attracted. I become tired and bored when I look at her. If Nkunzi likes a woman, I will have the feeling of wanting that woman all the time.

When I argue with Nkunzi about what he wants, whether it is with women or with my work as a healer, I will feel a weight pushing me down. Once, when I was walking up the steps to my consultation room I felt that somebody was pushing me and I fell. There was nobody there but I felt that I was being pushed. Then I heard a voice saying, "Don't ask questions. Just do as you are told." I told my trainer about it and she said "Now you know. If you are told to do something, don't ask. Do it."

I have tried to negotiate when Nkunzi chooses a woman I don't like. Sometimes I will pray and say, "No, I don't want that one. I don't want her, please." I will beg him and if he gets angry I have to make him *Ikhamba*[1] to please him, until he says he will choose another woman for me. I have to be really strong to resist what Nkunzi wants and usually I give in.

There was a certain woman who Nkunzi wanted as an ancestral wife, a *Nyankwabe*. The night before I met this woman at a sangoma ceremony, I had a dream about getting married. I was dressed in a man's fancy wedding clothes. I wore an *Imbatha*[2] around my chest and *isiphandla* around my upper arm. On my head there was an *umqhele*[3] and around my waist I had an *ibheshu*.[4] There were beads around my neck and I was carrying a spear and a shield.

The bride wore a blue shirt and an *ihwatha*[5] around her shoulders and on her head she wore *isiqhulo*.[6] I couldn't see her face because she was covered with a blanket. I was walking down the street with this woman. She was my bride.

We arrived at a certain place in a rural area and elder sangomas led us to a rondavel, which was lit by a circle of candles in all different colours. We were taken to a grass mat in the centre of the circle of candles and told to sit down. When we were seated, I lifted the blanket to look at my bride and found that she was an old woman. It gave me a terrible shock and I woke up in a panic.

The ceremony I attended the next day was held at the house of an elderly sangoma who also lived in Meadowlands. When I

---

1 African beer
2 Vest made of leather worn by Zulu men for ritual celebrations
3 Crown made of leopard skin
4 Apron made of leather, solid at the back and cut into strips in the front
5 Shawl
6 A tall, traditional hat with a flat top

arrived at the house many sangomas were already there. Normally the elders sit on a grass mat on one side and the sangomas who are beating the drums sit on a grass mat on the other side, and in the middle there will be a few chairs for the very respected elderly sangomas.

A young trainee led me to *isiqiki*[7] between two chairs for the great sangomas, and said, "You are supposed to sit here." I was very surprised because I had been given an important place. I thought she had made a mistake but she told me again, "This is where you must sit." So I sat between the two elders, wondering what was happening and why I had been given such a privileged place. While I was thinking about this, the old woman who was the owner of the house came towards me. She was carrying a blanket and she said, "You are Nkunzi?" And I said, "Yes, I am Nkunzi." She covered my shoulders with the blanket and the two elders on either side told me, "You are the chosen one. This is the woman you are going to marry." I looked at this old woman and shouted out, "No ways. I can't." I took off the blanket and ran home.

I went back to my consultation room and lit candles before communicating with Nkunzi. "Please, please, don't make me marry that old woman. I won't survive. Let me find you someone you will like. Don't make me marry that woman. Please." I begged him not to make me go through with the wedding but he was determined and I became very sick. I was exhausted and I had a headache. My joints ached and my body was so heavy that it was difficult for me to walk. I knew Nkunzi was punishing me.

After three days I went to my consultation room and I spoke to him again, "If you are going to kill me, who is going to work

---

7   A tree stump

for you? Let me be myself. Don't kill me now." That night he came to me in the form of a dream and he told me, "You don't have to stay with that woman or have sex with her. You just have to take the powers that she is giving you before she dies." And I said, "If it is like that, I will do what you say but don't say I should marry her." He said, "Just take the powers that she is giving you."

After a few days I went back to the old woman's house and I talked to her. Her name was Jabulisile, which means "bringer of joy." Nkunzi had appeared in her dreams and told her that he wanted her as a wife and she must leave her powers with me. She told me, "There are things I have to leave with you." She had to perform another ceremony. This time I was prepared.

Again she covered herself with a blanket after dressing me in the traditional dress I had dreamed about and giving me a shield and a spear. We danced and while we were dancing I felt Nkunzi's spirit in me. Afterwards I went into Jabulisile's room. Two elderly men were waiting there for me. They gave me guidance and prepared me to receive the old woman's powers when she passed away. They also gave me two of the bones from her bag to include in my bag.

So that day I took Jabulisile as an ancestral wife. Each time I went to a ceremony after this she was there, but she was sick. I could see she was sick. I felt pity for her and I started to have a bond with her. When it was her turn to dance I was the one beating the drum for her and I assisted her to get dressed. We were looking after each other and she taught me about some herbs and ways of healing. I knew it was because Nkunzi wanted to increase my knowledge and understanding.

When Jabulisile passed away, her family called me and I went with them and buried her. We did a ceremony and a cleansing and

I collected some more of her things, including some traditional cloths.

Jabulisile gives me that feminine side and when she is with me I feel kindness towards people. She makes me want to dance in female clothes and I enjoy that moment when I feel that part of myself. It makes me feel love for my womanhood. But Nkunzi is much stronger and when he is around I want to dress in trousers and be a man. Nkunzi feels naked in a dress.

With Jabulisile my sexuality is not affected. I don't feel like having sex when she is around. The only thing that I feel like doing is helping people. She brings me pregnant clients. That is how I will know that she is with me. There will be many pregnant clients all coming on the same day and I will heal them. The person who loves sex is Nkunzi, and he definitely loves it.

In traditional Zulu culture, a man must be a man and do male things and a woman must be a woman and do female things but with sangomas it is more flexible. I can dance like a woman and wear a woman's clothes and dance like a man and wear a man's clothes. I can do the work of a man, like slaughtering a goat or a cow, although in traditional Zulu culture a woman cannot slaughter. As long as I have respect for the animal that is being slaughtered, I can do the work of a man. Sometimes I become too much of a man and people will look at me and say, "Today you look like a man." That is when I know it is Nkunzi's spirit in me. If I am just myself then I am not too much of a man, I am feminine too. Then I know it's me.

When clients come to see me I will change depending on what the client needs. If I have a client who is a woman, the spirit that will come to me will be a female spirit and I will be in a female spirit assisting that female client. But when I have got a male client I am going to have a male ancestor in me and I myself will be in the male side in me. I can tell even by the things I do. When I have done something I will think, gosh, this was supposed to be done by a man or this was supposed to be done by a woman. I see the actions and facially my expressions change.

When my grandmother, my mom's mother, is with me, I will use the Bible instead of the bones. I will hear her spirit saying to me, "Go to the Bible" then I will take out the Bible and pray. After praying, when I open the Bible I will be able to diagnose a client's sickness. I won't see what is written in the Bible, I will see the person's problem. The Bible is like a mirror or a TV for me. Somebody who sees me may think I am reading the words in the Bible but I am looking at a picture that is shown to me and I will be able to say, "This is the problem." If the problem is in the client's leg, I will see the leg and see where the blockage is. Then I will focus on what I see and ask, "What is the cause of this? How shall I help this person?" The ancestors will give me all the instructions.

Sometimes I see what is happening to somebody by becoming disturbed and confused and if a client comes to me it is like I am the one who is having that problem. For example, if a client is going to be attacked, I will see myself being attacked. I become confused. Is this something that is going to happen in the future or something that is in the past? Then a client arrives and begs me, "Please help me. I have been attacked." It is devastating because it feels to me that I have been attacked. Normally I check the bones and see if it is going to happen to me or if somebody else is coming with that problem. Then the bones will tell me, it is somebody else's problem. Then I am prepared. I get a sense of what the problem is before the client arrives.

At other times I will dream that I am the one who is sick and I feel sickness in my own body. Part of what I do as a healer is to feel in my own body what is happening to somebody else. I will have pains in my own body. For example, I might wake up with pains in my body and feeling weak and that I want to vomit, and when I check the bones I will find out that there is a child who is sick and very weak. Then the next day or a few days later a woman will arrive with her child who is weak and vomiting and I will be prepared. I will know what I need to do with the child. When I give the herbs to the client, the symptoms disappear from my own body. Not all sangomas do this. Some just catch a headache and then they know someone is coming and they just check the bones and see that someone is coming and what kind of problem they will have. For me it is worse.

Sometimes the ancestors show me in a dream. I will dream of a person with certain symptoms or I will dream that I have the symptoms and the next day a person will arrive with the same symptoms. Once I dreamed that I was sick and in the morning a man arrived with the symptoms I dreamed about. He had been poisoned at work. When I looked at him I saw that he had turned purple. His whole body was the colour purple and I told him, "I can't help you." He cried, "Please help me." He was begging me. I didn't know what to do. When I looked at him I could see that he was going to die. Suddenly I felt dizzy and I heard a voice saying, "Take this herb and this herb." The voice was giving instructions. I closed my eyes and automatically took the herbs off the shelves. I didn't even look at what I was doing. I did all this with my eyes closed. I combined the herbs and gave them to him and told him, "Drink this." After he had drunk it I told him to go home and sleep. As he was leaving the room he started to vomit. I helped him and took him home. Four days later he came back and he was completely recovered. He asked me, "How did you mix the herbs with your eyes closed?" I said, "I don't know."

There is also a baby ancestor who comes to me. I think it is one of my mother's sisters who died when she was a baby. When she comes I want to play before doing my work. I normally ask her to go and call the elders or deliver messages to them. If she is around you will see me eating a lot of sweets and playing.

Snake power helps me to sense where sickness has started, whether in the bone marrow or in the blood or somewhere else in the body. With the snake I can see where the sickness started and where it goes. I feel when the snake is in me. It takes over and I take the form of a snake and I move this way and that way until I can identify the cause of the sickness.

Nkunzi is more powerful than all the other ancestors for me. He helps me with the most difficult cases, especially with men. After becoming a sangoma, I learned more about how to work with my ancestors, especially with Nkunzi. I was not ashamed of being a lesbian and a sangoma and I did not hide who I was. I was proud to be a Zulu lesbian. I felt that I was pure because I was not contaminated by sex with a man.

CHAPTER SEVEN

In Search of Community

MPUMELELO (MPUMI) NJINGE was a gay South African film maker from Kwa Thema. He was very active in the lesbian and gay community. When I met him in 2002 he was doing research for a documentary film about three lesbian sangomas for the Gay and Lesbian Archives (GALA). I was at a sangoma ceremony and after I finished dancing, my girlfriend came and sat on my lap. She was rubbing my shoulders when Mpumi approached me. He was surprised because we were open about our same-sex sexuality in a ceremony where all the other sangomas were straight or hiding their sexuality. He questioned me about this. I told him, "When I grew up I was not in the closet so why should I put my life in a closet now?" He told me about his research on same-sex sangomas and asked if I was interested. I told him I was very interested so he took me to meet Ruth Morgan, the director of GALA.

Meeting Ruth in January 2002 changed my life. Ruth was the new director at GALA when I met her. She was working with Mpumi Njinge and another director, Paolo Alberton, on the film called, *Everything Must Come to Light*. The film was about older lesbian sangomas so I didn't qualify but I was in the background in some of the scenes.

One of the first things I said to Ruth was, "I want to write a book about my life." Maybe because I know I won't have children to talk about me after I die, it has been a dream since I was a child to have my own book. I told Ruth, "If there is a book about me, I will be remembered." Ruth said she would try and help me but first she asked me to get involved in the project to interview same-sex sangomas for six months. I was very happy to accept. I worked with Busi Kheswa, who works full-time for GALA, finding and interviewing same-sex sangomas.

The research was used in many different ways and it took me on my first trip out of South Africa. In 2004 I went to Ireland with Ruth to present the research at a lesbian conference in Dublin. Mpumi Njinge died in the same year that I began to work for GALA. He died of AIDS-related illnesses. We showed *Everything Must Come to Light*, the film that Mpumi co-directed, at the conference. People were surprised to see me in my traditional sangoma clothes and to hear about same-sex sangomas. I felt proud to be associated with an organisation like GALA because of the role it plays in empowering gay and lesbian people in South Africa.

Before going to Ireland, Ruth also got me involved in the African Women's Life Story project that GALA did for the Sex and Secrecy Conference held at Wits University. Participants came from six countries in eastern and southern Africa. We participated in a workshop in which we were trained to do same-sex life story research. My research focused on female sangomas who have taken female ancestral wives. We prepared a presentation of our research findings in another workshop just before the conference. After the conference I co-wrote a chapter on my research for the book *Tommy Boys, Lesbian Men and*

Ancestral Wives: Female Same-Sex Practices in Africa.[1] Since 2002, Ruth has been a mentor to me. I call her "mother" because she is always watching out for me and giving me opportunities.

When I first started interviewing same-sex sangomas for GALA, I was nervous. I had a strong need to be connected to other lesbian sangomas because for a long time I had felt completely alone. I wanted to live my life as a sangoma and a lesbian – as one person – not divided up into pieces and I wanted to connect with other lesbian sangomas who felt the same way. Although I was confident as a lesbian I was not confident as a lesbian sangoma. I didn't know how the sangomas I met were going to react to me when I told them I was out. Would they reject me? Would they stone me? Would they chase me away? These thoughts were in my mind because I knew that many of these sangomas were still living in hiding. They were not public about their sexuality like me. Many people believe that being lesbian is not African. Sangomas are afraid to come out because of this. There are people who say that if you are lesbian you cannot have the powers to heal and others believe that being homosexual is a sin. That is why most same-sex sangomas feel that if they disclose their status they will lose their clients.

The first person I interviewed was an older lesbian sangoma called Bongiwe, who was in her forties. I spoke to her on the phone to set up an appointment. I didn't know what to expect when I met her because she had a man's voice. There was nothing feminine in her voice. Bongiwe stayed in a flat in Braamfontein with her partner. I went up in a shaky old lift with a metal gate. The security guard came with me to show me the way.

---

[1] Morgan, R. and Wieringa, S. *Tommy Boys, Lesbian Men and Ancestral Wives: Female Same-Sex Practices in Africa*. Johannesburg: Jacana Media, 2005.

I knocked on the door and immediately recognised the voice that shouted out, "It's open! Come in!" I went in and the security guy came with me. He called out to Bongiwe, asking for a glass of water and she shouted back, "Take a beer out of the fridge." I could see that the security guard was at home in Bongiwe's flat. He opened the fridge and took a beer. After he left and I stood in the small kitchen waiting for Bongiwe, not knowing what to expect. I thought she would be butch because of her voice on the phone. But I was surprised to find her dressed in feminine clothes, a white T-shirt and a skirt with flowers on it and a sangoma cloth wrapped around her. She was barefoot. The first thing I noticed was that she had breasts and a beard like a man who has just shaved. I was impressed by her way of expressing the male and the female in her at the same time.

Bongiwe and her partner live in a small flat with a kitchen and a bathroom and in between an open space that is divided up with curtains into a lounge and a bedroom and Bongiwe's consultation room. I spent three or four hours doing the interview. It was fascinating for me to meet somebody who had that "tsotsi taal" in her and a mannish look, somebody who had a moustache and a beard and that ghetto life in her. When she was speaking I could see that she was a lesbian who is strong in herself. She gave me courage and confidence.

Bongiwe's feelings for girls were with her from childhood. She told me, "While I was playing with other children, I'll have my own wife and I'll sleep with a girl. I will tell her not to tell others and it would be our secret. That is where I started to sleep with girls."

Only her brother understood. One day he asked her, "Why are you so rough?" Bongiwe replied, "Maybe I am a boy."

Bongiwe was forced into a marriage after a boy took her

In Search of Community

[handwritten note at top: "always try to decide if veins are trans or lesbian !!!"]

by force when she was still in school. After he raped her, this boy paid lobola[2] for her and there was nothing she could do. While she was married, an old man appeared to Bongiwe in a vision and he told her he did not want her to have another man. After this, whenever her husband tried to have sex with her, she would immediately begin to menstruate. She menstruated for three years – day and night – without stopping. Eventually her husband went to visit a sangoma in Alex with his mother and the sangoma told him Bongiwe had *Mundawu*[3] (see next page) sitting in her womb. After this her husband's family began to say he should take *isithembu*[4] and Bongiwe was free.

Before Bongiwe was born, her mother was told by a prophet that she would give birth to a baby girl with spiritual gifts and even when she was a child Bongiwe knew what was going to happen before it happened. She attended the Zionist Christian Church and when she was still at school she started to have visions. She saw an old man telling her he would come back for her in three days' time and she should pack her things. When he appeared to her again three days later, Bongiwe left without saying goodbye and with only five rands in her pocket. She got into a taxi without knowing where she was going but the old man was with her and he guided her to a street where she heard *intshomane*, the sound of drums beating. At that time she had never seen sangomas before and she sat down on a rock to watch what they were doing. While she was sitting there a young boy came to her and said. "It is a long time I have been waiting for you. You must come and take your bag." So Bongiwe followed him to her trainer.

---

2 Dowry paid by a Zulu man to the family of his bride
3 Ancestors, not necessarily from a family line
4 A second wife

Bongiwe's ancestor is her mother's grandfather who was a chief. She and her ancestor love the same woman. This woman is Bongiwe's wife and also her ancestor's wife. She told me: "I proposed to her and she agreed. I went to her place... I told her mother that I want to marry her daughter and she said, there was nothing to say; I should just do as I wished. We went to look for the rings and went to the pastor to bless our rings. We got married and I left home and I came to stay in a flat with her. I bought the blankets to present to her ancestors... My partner is an ancestral wife and she is my wife. I paid lobola to the ancestors for her. I bought clothes for the ancestors of and *Mnguni*,[5] I bought chickens and I made *Ikhamba*. I bought gin and brandy. I bought another blanket for her to wear so that she could be able to help me with ancestral things... If I am busy and I want a certain *muthi*[6] or I want something in the *ndumba*[7], she must be able to fetch it. Or if I am sick, she should be able to prepare an *imbiza*[8] for a patient."

Bongiwe's sex life with her partner is also her ancestor's sex life: "I thought this thing I am doing is my own but when I was busy training, I realized that this person is doing what I am doing but he is inside me. So I experienced right here that these people are doing what is in me, what I like. It's because this person is in me. Even if he does not come in a physical form, but he is in me."

While Bongiwe was telling me about how she met her partner, her partner walked in. She was much younger than Bongiwe. At first I thought she was Bongiwe's daughter. She was dressed in

---

5 Ancestors from a family line
6 Traditional remedy
7 Shrine
8 Pot of medicine

a nurse's uniform. Her partner called her "Baba". Sangomas are always called "Baba" by their trainees and by other sangomas. It means, "father." Being called "father" is the highest form of respect in African culture. The greatest one is always masculine. I asked her, "Is this a trainee?" And she replied, "No. This is my partner, Lindi." Lindi came over to Bongiwe and they kissed. She had long, relaxed hair and a slim body. Lindi opened the curtain to the part of the room where they slept and took off her uniform. She tied a sangoma cloth around her waist and then she went over to the fridge and took out a beer. She had bare breasts and obviously felt free in front of me. I was fascinated because both women were so free.

After the interview, Bongiwe and Lindi asked me to stay the night. They said other same-sex sangomas would be coming over. I couldn't stay because I hadn't informed my partner but I so happy to be welcomed into their flat whenever I wanted to come over. Bongiwe said, "Come back tomorrow then. Bring your partner. Come whenever you like."

When I left Bongiwe's place, there was a big smile on my face. I felt connected. I had made new friends and I had an idea of what it can be like to live the life of a lesbian sangoma in Johannesburg, spontaneously and freely.

* * *

I had this confidence in me after meeting Bongiwe and I went out and found other lesbian sangomas. I travelled to the areas where people lived and interviewed them in their homes. In six months I interviewed more than 30 sangomas and discovered that I was part of a community of same-sex sangomas in urban and rural areas, from Soweto to all the provinces of South Africa. Many of the people I interviewed have kept their sexual identities secret and did not want their names used. For this reason, most of the names of people I interviewed have been changed.

I was introduced to Sindi by Bongiwe. I interviewed her in her house in Daveyton. I travelled by taxi and got lost so I phoned her on her cell and she came to fetch me from the bus stop. She said she would be wearing *injiti*[9] so I saw her from a distance. We walked to Sindi's RDP house. It is a one-bedroom house with an asbestos roof. There was a peach tree in the yard.

One thing I noticed immediately about Sindi is that she was a person full of sorrow. She wasn't bitter but she was not a happy person. She was like someone who is missing something or someone. I found my intuition was not flowing so well when I was with her so I called on my ancestors to help me but they didn't come. I felt that it was because there was something missing in Sindi. There was not enough power in her. One thing that came out in the interview is that she has a child of rape. She never talked much about the child and I could see she wanted to protect the child so I didn't ask her. I didn't want to open that wound that was inside her.

Sindi's father was not around when she was born and because her mother was a domestic worker she was left with her grandmother who is deaf and paralysed. So Sindi always had to help out in the house and with bringing up her younger brothers and sisters.

At school, Sindi's friends were boys and she used to play soccer and fight like a boy. She said she was never fascinated by beauty. She used to go bare foot and cut her hair very short so

---

9 Traditional cloth

that she was like a boy.

She had a dream to be a teacher and she was clever in school but after completing primary school, she couldn't proceed with her schooling because there was no money. She told me how hard it was to live in that house, especially because her uncles were not kind to her and her brothers and sisters and since her grandmother was disabled she could not protect them:

"We would sometimes go without food. We used to take plastics when we went to school and pick up coal from the street so that we would be able to make a fire and cook. We grew up very poor. It was worse for me because I was the oldest. I saw everything that was happening to my young brother and sister and I used to get angry. Sometimes (my uncles) would insult them and it was not nice. But on the other hand my grandmother loved us."

Like me, Sindi was initiated into the lesbian life by an older woman. The woman was the wife of a priest. She was 38 years old and Sindi was 16 when the woman asked Sindi's grandmother if Sindi could sleep over at her place one New Year's Eve because her husband and children were gone to the homelands for a visit. That is when Sindi learned about being a lesbian.

When she was 18 things started happening to Sindi that she didn't understand. She would dream things, like that somebody would die, and it would happen. Sindi's grandmother was a prophet and she told Sindi she also had the gift of prophecy. There were no sangomas on her mother's side so Sindi did not like sangomas very much. When she came across one she would walk in the opposite direction.

After she started getting very sick a woman appeared to Sindi in a dream and asked her, "Do you want to live?" Sindi said, "Yes. I want to live." Then the woman in the dream said, "If you want to live you must do what I say," and she handed her some beads. When Sindi told her grandmother about the dream she said she didn't know what they could do because there had never been a sangoma in the family and there was no money to pay for the training.

To pay for the training, Sindi had to do hard jobs for her trainer and she had to stay at her trainer's place for two years. She was also raped by her trainer's brother and she got pregnant.

After leaving training, Sindi lived the life of a lesbian. She has a relationship with a woman called Vumidlozi and she also has an ancestral wife for her male ancestor, Masango. She told me:

"There are times when I feel that I am a man, then I will know that my ancestor is in my blood. He has a woman that belongs to the ancestor. Her name is Dudu. When the ancestor is here he will want Dudu to be around to prepare water and to dress me. As she is doing all these things to me she is actually doing them to Nsangu. Nsangu chose his woman and I chose mine. I love Vumidlozi and she is the woman for me. Dudu does not know about Vumidlozi but she can see we are always together. She only comes to see if the ancestor is okay and to see that all my clothes are clean."

Sindi didn't negotiate the choice of woman with her ancestor. She was told by her ancestor that he had chosen Dudu, who is still a young girl of 13. After hearing what her ancestor said, Sindi went to the girl's parents to tell them that their child has been chosen by the ancestors and how things would be from then on. The ancestor told Sindi that the money she makes as a sangoma must also be used to care for the ancestral wife, so she lives like a man with two wives.

When I left I felt upset about a 13-year-old being taken as an ancestral wife. I think it is too much to give a child the duties of an ancestral wife. That child will never have time to play. I felt

 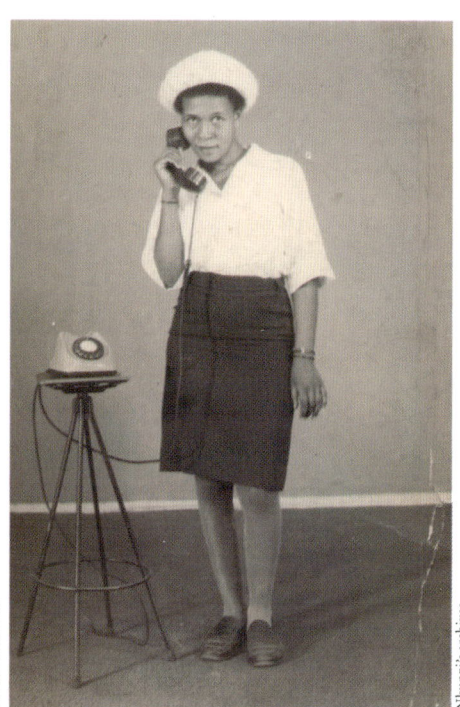

My father and mother posing at a studio in Jo'burg city

At age 3 on my grandfather's car in Meadowlands

This is me, age 17, a student at Veritas Secondary School and already out

Me on the left in a white dress, with my sisters and children from the neighbourhood

With my grandfather, Isaac Nkabinde, outside the house in Meadowlands

This still, from *Everything Must Come to Light*, directed by Paulo Alberton and Mpumi Njinge and produced by GALA, shows a muthi market

The Drakensburg Mountains in rural KwaZulu-Natal

Leaving my trainer's house after 8 months of training

After graduation as a sangoma with a fellow trainee

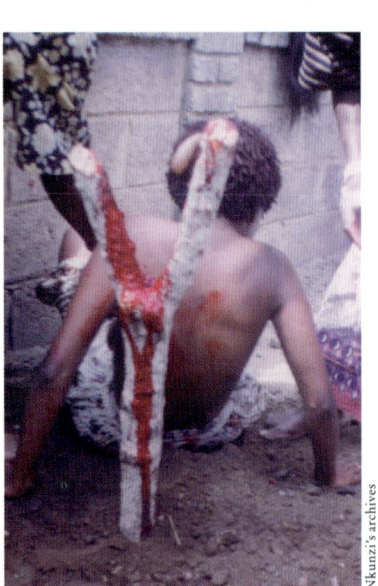

Sealing the *iphande* after entering my parents' home as a sign to the ancestors that they are welcome

The *iphande* outside the house

Doing a reading for a client

In my sangoma clothes, in the street outside my house

With a client in my consulting room

Throwing the bones

Muthi

My consulting room

With Busi at GALA

With Ruth at GALA

At Constitution Hill, with an image of Gandhi in the background

[handwritten top: agency moved away from you]

angry and upset. Sindi's ancestors have robbed that child of her childhood, just like Sindi was robbed of her childhood. I think Sindi should have fought with her ancestors and told them, "The person you have chosen is still a child!" That child has to help in the consultation room and look after the room when Sindi is away finding herbs. It is limiting her youth days. Nkunzi chose an older woman and even then I negotiated with him. I didn't just accept. The ancestors are not deaf. They will listen and they can compromise. I believe the ancestors do give you a chance to suggest something else. [handwritten: can control life]

Probably Dudu's parents respected the ancestors and were afraid that something would happen to their child. Also they probably needed the money. Sindi and the child's parents should have got together and made a compromise for the ancestors because that child will suffer.

For me Sindi did not strike me as a sangoma, as a healer. She was too full of sadness and I couldn't feel her ancestors' power.

[handwritten: depression?]

* * *

I interviewed Masechaba in her consultation room, a backroom at her grandmother's place in Sebokeng. She was about 31 when I met her. We took off our shoes outside the consultation room and sat on a grass mat for the interview. There were wooden shelves all along the wall with her herbs on them and on one side a shrine made of grass.

When I arrived at the house, there were quite a few cars parked outside. They might have been Masechaba's clients. She told me that she sees the same clients who come to her every month. I remembered what my trainer said, "If your client comes again and again there is something wrong with your work." Masechaba was very butch and very proud. She was a Mapantsula style, tsotsi person.

Masechaba's mother died after giving birth to her. She also lived with her grandmother and grew up in poverty. She was only 12 when she got the ancestral calling. She was alone in the house preparing for school one day when lightning struck the house and hit her.

Her grandmother found her lying on the floor and she screamed for help, thinking she was dead. The neighbours came and an old man was called to give his opinion. He told Masechaba's grandmother that the child was not dead but her ancestors were calling her. Masechaba's grandmother was puzzled and she said, "She is young, this can't happen." The old man asked if he could take Masechaba away for a few days and because she was desperate her grandmother agreed.

On the fourth day Masechaba woke up and the old man sent someone to tell her grandmother that she was alive. The old man started treating her with herbs to make her strong and in the morning a female goat was slaughtered and she drank the blood. After that the drumming began to awaken and revive Masechaba's ancestors.

She stayed in training for four years because her grandmother had trouble finding money to take her out of initiation. Masechaba's granny was hurt every time she went to visit her granddaughter because sangomas were not from her side of the family. The sangoma calling came from her father's side and that part of the family never cared about Masechaba. Her story made me think about my own father because even though he was not around, he was hurt and angry because my ancestor, Nkunzi, is from my mother's side.

For Masechaba church is still very important. She believes in church a lot but she no longer goes to church services because the church that she belonged to does not approve of sangomas. She is confused by the church's attitude to her. She said, "With me, I didn't choose to be called by the ancestors. I can't compare God and ancestors. God is powerful and mighty and the ancestors are powerful because God gave them power. It is even in the Bible that God gave the prophets power to help people. God is God and the ancestors are ancestors."

I agreed with what she said. We pray first to God and then to the ancestors. The herbs and everything we use come from God.

Masechaba does not have a male ancestor influencing her sexuality. She works with male and female ancestors. She found out about being a lesbian after completing her training but she was always a tomboy. Her family didn't have a problem with her sexuality because her granny informed them that her parents had left her with a girl who will grow up being a boy. It was always that way and she knew it from the beginning.

Masechaba told me she sees more than 140 clients a months. I think she sees the same clients over and over again. This is a problem. People can easily become dependent on sangomas and spend all their money going back about the same thing because of fear.

Masechaba is out as a lesbian. She is very tough. I think her life made her tough from a young age. Even though her community does not accept her sexuality they still come to her as a sangoma. She doesn't care about the opinions of other people. She said, "It matters not what they say about lesbians and gay people. I live my life to the fullest." I felt that Masechaba had power as a lesbian but I wasn't sure about her work as a sangoma.

* * *

I met Mashudu at a sangoma ceremony in Braam Fischer. I told her I was interviewing lesbian sangomas. She told me she had a story to tell me but she was not ready yet. After waiting about three weeks, I called her. She put me off and said, "I will call you when I am ready." Four months later she called me and said, "Can we meet?" She asked if she could come over to my house. I said, "Yes, of course that is fine." I was surprised to see the change in her appearance. She had lost of a lot of weight and her bones were sticking out. I could tell that she was sick but I didn't ask any questions. We sat in silence for quite a long time. I was waiting for her to tell me why she wanted to see me. I was hoping to interview her but again she said she was not ready to give me the details. It was a Friday and we decided to go to a sangoma ceremony that we both knew about so we left my house without an interview and went to the place where the ceremony was taking place. We spent the weekend there and on Sunday when we came back to my place she told me she was going to the family farm in Venda and she would call me from there. It was very mysterious. I couldn't understand what was happening in her. There was nothing I could do but wait for Mashudu to tell me her story.

A few weeks later I phoned her again. This time she asked if I knew how to get to Venda. I told her my brother-in-law knew the place and he was planning a visit so I could get a lift with him. She gave me directions to a certain shop in Thoyandou and said that the shop owner was a family member and he would show me the way. It is about two and a half hours drive to Thoyandou. Mashudu's directions were clear and we found the shop easily. My sister and brother-in-law dropped me of at the shop and I arranged to call them when I was finished with the interview. The shop was one of those all purpose shops that you find in rural areas. There was a man and a young boy inside. I told them I had come to see Mashudu and the man took me in his car to Mashudu's place.

It was a large house on a big plot. The houses were quite a distance away from each other and there were patches of veld in between. It was already getting dark when we arrived. We went in through the kitchen door and found a young woman there in her early twenties. It was a big kitchen with old furniture and a coal stove. The man spoke to the young woman in Venda and then he said goodbye and left. The young woman offered me some tea. While I was sitting there waiting for her to prepare the tea, my cell phone rang. It was Mashudu. She asked where I was. I told her I was in the kitchen in her house. She said I should tell the young woman to take me to her room.

I followed the young woman down a long passage and she opened the door of a room on the other side of the house. The curtains were drawn and it was dark inside. I could just make out a double bed with lots of blankets on it and next to it a table with many bottles and packets of tablets on it. "Hello, Nkunzi." Mashudu's voice came from inside the blankets but I couldn't see her. She told me to sit down on a chair next to the bed. I moved towards the bed and sat down. I could hardly recognise Mashudu. Her eyes were popping out of her head. She was very thin and she looked as if she was dying. Her cheeks were hollow and her skin was a grayish colour. Her face was wet and her dreads were full of sweat. I greeted her. Without greeting me back she said, "Did you bring your tape?" I nodded and took it out of my bag. Mashudu told the young woman to leave us alone. The young woman went out on tiptoe and closed the door very softly behind her. I got the tape recorder ready and was about to start the interview when Mashudu said, "Check if the woman is in the kitchen then ask her to go and buy some more milk. As she goes out, lock the door." I went to the kitchen and took some money out of my pocket and asked the young woman to please go and buy some milk for Mashudu. She left and I locked the door as Mashudu told me. When I went back to the room, I told Mashudu, "I won't ask you questions because you know what you want to say. Just talk."

Mashudu was born in Venda and came to live in Pimville in Soweto when she was 13. She was a normal girl who liked to play with other girls and boys. She enjoyed playing house and always wanted to be the mother. There was a girl staying in the same street as her, named Zinhle. Zinhle was a tomboy and she looked like a boy. When she came to play, Mashudu would be the wife and Zinhle would be the husband. One day when the two girls were playing house and sleeping in a shack they had made, Zinhle kissed Mashudu and from that day she knew that she would love women not men. The girls ended up at the same boarding school for their matric year and their affair continued until they completed their schooling and Zinhle went to KZN and Mashudu went to the Pretoria Technikon to study art.

When she was in her second year at the Pretoria Technikon, Mashudu's legs began to swell and she felt as if she was losing her mind. Her mother took her to a sangoma in Mfolo who said she must go for training but because she grew up going to the Roma church,[10] she didn't believe what the sangoma was saying and after being cured, she ran away from home and went to stay with her lover, Nelly, for two years.

After this Mashudu became sick again. This time it was much

---

10 Roman Catholic Church

worse and she couldn't walk. Her family carried her to Venda to another sangoma and she was told by this man if she did not agree to go for training she would never walk again, so she went into training immediately.

Mashudu has four ancestors, three women and one man. Her female ancestor, Takalani Mbabale was her main ancestor. She was Mashudu's great grandmother from her father's side. She told me that this ancestor loved her womanhood and she made Mashudu a full woman.

After she graduated as a sangoma, the man who was her trainer told Mashudu that her ancestors wanted him to marry her. He already had seven wives and 16 children and he wanted to make Mashudu his eighth wife. Mashudu told him to wait seven days for her ancestors to come to her personally and she made him promise that if they didn't come in seven days he would take her back home. He agreed and after seven days she told the man that her ancestors wanted her to return home. Her trainer kept his promise and he called her family and arranged a date for her to return home.

While she was waiting for her family to come and fetch her, Mashudu's trainer came into the room where she was sleeping one night and burned a sleeping potion which made Mashudu fall into a deep sleep. In the middle of the night she found the man on top of her and she couldn't scream or do anything because she felt so weak and powerless. Her trainer told her that if she told her family about the rape they would not believe her because his wives know that that she is running after him like all the *amathwasa*[11] who come to him for training are running after him. From that day Mashudu hated all men.

---

11 Trainees, literally "children of the ancestors"

Mashudu was 23 when she returned to Soweto and began to live the life of a lesbian sangoma. She had a partner called Ntuthuko. When Mashudu and her partner both became sick with "non-stop 'flu," Ntuthuko said they should go for an HIV test but Mashudu refused. She said, "Why should I go. I myself am a healer." When Ntuthuko went for the test she discovered she was HIV-positive. The two women had a fight, each accusing the other of being unfaithful. Ntuthuko was so upset that she committed suicide by hanging herself. She left a note swearing that she had always been faithful to Mashudu and would always love her.

After Ntuthuko's funeral, Mashudu went back to her family's farm in Venda. When she arrived there she discovered that her trainer was sick with full-blown AIDS. All of his wives were dead and out of 16, all except three of his children had died.

Mashudu's heart was filled with sorrow and anger. She went into the room where her trainer was sleeping and after closing all the windows and doors, she turned on the gas from the gas stove, knowing that the man would light a candle in the night. After doing this she wiped away her fingerprints and left the house.

In the morning when she woke up she heard that her trainer had been admitted to the hospital because his room had burned down. His children died in the fire. Mashudu told me, "I never told anyone about this but because I can see I'm going to die now, I want you to do whatever you like with my story."

I felt pity for Mashudu. She told me, "I was a churchgoer before I became a sangoma. I was a child who was baptized in the Roman Catholic Church, but when I went for training to be a sangoma I stopped going to church. Now I ask myself, why did the ancestor and God – if they exist – let that man rape me?

And again, why did they let me get infected when I finally found peace in my life, finding someone who loves me? I just want to know from them, why did they let this bad luck come to my side? So my belief to both is already dead."

She blamed God and ancestors for not protecting her and for sending her to a place where she got her death. It made me sad. She had that anger in her against God and ancestors. Why did the ancestors allow it to happen? In her case, I don't know who is to blame. If it was me I suppose I would definitely blame the ancestors but I would look at the path I have taken and ask if my ancestors were testing my strength. Whatever happens in life, I always ask myself, "Will I let it overcome me or be a fighter and conquer it?"

About the murder, I understand that she wanted revenge. I don't think it is okay to take somebody's life but she felt it would calm her senses and put her at ease. She had this thing in her, this secret inside her. If she had talked out about it, she could still be alive. She was near to death when I saw her.

I think she made many wrong decisions in her life. I think she misunderstood her calling. She went to the wrong person for her training. She didn't seek more clarification. She went to the person who healed her but he was not necessarily the one she was supposed to go to for training. She had the ancestors on top of her and she couldn't walk but she didn't wait for her ancestors to point out the way to go. She just went with that man because she wanted to walk. In my case, if I get a client who has a problem with his or her ancestors I will cure the client first. If the client says she or he wants me to train them, I say, "No, no, no! They didn't choose me. Wait for the ancestors to choose for you and to show you the right person to train you." The person who heals you is not always the person who must train you.

In my case I recognised my trainer from a dream. When I saw her I knew that I was supposed to be trained by her. But, I also knew that I was not supposed to eat her herbs. The herbs I had to eat came from another healer. My trainer also knew that she only had to train me and the herbs she had to give me would not be her herbs. My ancestors appeared to my trainer in a dream and told her she must not give me her herbs and she was shown where to get the herbs for me. If I had eaten my trainer's herbs, nothing would have worked out for me. She followed the rules and she even said to me, "You are not supposed to eat my herbs. This is what I am going to do." Another healer, a man who my trainer knew, came with the herbs that were right for me. These were the herbs that Nkunzi had chosen for me. If you choose your own path and don't follow the path that is chosen for you by your ancestors, something will definitely go wrong.

* * *

I saw Fefe and her partner at a ceremony in Soweto. I could tell that they were definitely lesbians but I checked with a gay friend, Sam, and he confirmed that Fefe was a lesbian so I approached her and asked if I could make a time to speak to her. Fefe is from Piet Retief but she was spending a month in Johannesburg for some sangoma business, so I arranged to meet her at Sam's house.

When she was growing up, Fefe was somebody who liked to isolate herself from other children. She came from a big family. In the house there was her mother, her father, her grandfather, Fefe and her four sisters.

She used to play by herself and after school and nearly every day she played in the family graveyard. She was always by herself. One day she fell asleep on top of somebody's grave when she was pretending the grave was her bed. She dreamed of somebody asking her to accompany him to a sangoma ceremony. She couldn't see the person's face but she could hear a man's voice. When Fefe and the man arrived at the ceremony, in her dream, he gave her sangoma clothes to wear and asked her to dance with him. After dancing he gave her two bones and he told her she should go to Nhlazatshe, to a woman there who was going to teach her how to use the bones. She still wears these bones, one around her neck and the other around her wrist, even today.

When Fefe woke up, she ran home. When she arrived at home she opened her hands and found that she was holding the two bones from her dream in her hands. She didn't know what to do with them so she put them in her school bag and the next day she told a friend from school, Dumazile, what had happened. She even showed her the bones. After school she took Dumazile to the graveyard to show her the grave she fell asleep on. Dumazile told Fefe to tell her mother but she was afraid so she didn't say anything.

A month later Fefe started to hear voices in her ears and see shadows around her face and she had a feeling that someone was watching her. Her grandmother asked her what was wrong and she told her the whole story. Fefe's granny spoke to her mother and said they must talk to the ancestors and find out what they want. So they made a ceremony by slaughtering a goat and talking to the ancestors.

That night, Fefe heard the voice of the man from her dream again, telling her to go with him. She went to Nhlazatshe in a trance. She didn't remember going there but when she woke up that is where she was, in a strange house. When the owner of the house came, Fefe recognised her from her dreams. She told Fefe she had been waiting for her for a long time. Fefe asked her,

"How did I get here?" Her trainer said, "Your ancestors showed you the way," and she sent a message to Fefe's family to say that she was at the place for *ekuthwaseni*.[12] Fefe's family came and asked her if she was ready to do the training. Fefe told them she wanted to go back to finish school. The old lady spoke to Fefe's ancestors, telling them that she would go back to school. Then she said to Fefe, "Do not forget that you have to take your grandfather's gift."

After passing her exams, Fefe went to boarding school in uMlazi to do her matric. There she became close to another lesbian called Nomsa and they became secret lovers until after the matric exams.

A few years later, after Fefe's father passed away, she started hearing the voices again. One day she woke up and told her mother she had to go to Nhlazatshe to fulfill her promise to the trainer. When she arrived there they prepared everything. They lay down *amacansi*[13] and made her sit down in the middle and they covered her in white sheets and *amabhayi*,[14] then they started beating the drums. The next thing, Fefe found herself sitting in a room with four other sangomas. The old lady told her that her ancestor had come out and his name was Mahlabezulu and from now on her name was dead and she must be called by her ancestor's name. Fefe's mother, her grandmother and her sisters came to say goodbye and she stayed with her trainer for a whole two years.

When she was getting ready to go home, Fefe's trainer had a ceremony for all her grandchildren. The ceremony was on a

---

12 Training as a sangoma
13 Grass mats
14 Cloths that are wound around a new trainee

Sunday and the trainer's grandchildren arrived on a Friday. One of the grandchildren came from Egoli. Her name was Mzusephi. She was tall and tough and she looked like a boy. By that time Fefe was 24 and Mzusephi was 21. Fefe was so attracted to Mzusephi that she found herself looking at her without blinking. Fefe's trainer saw her looking at her grandchild and in the afternoon when it was time for *ukushonisa*[15] she hid that grandchild of hers for Fefe. Fefe had to call out to her ancestors to tell her what has been hidden and she found that it was Mzusephi that her trainer had hidden.

Fefe's ancestor told her trainer that he wanted Mzuzephi to marry Fefe and that she should not marry a man. After Fefe found Mzusephi, her trainer took the two girls to her *endumbshe*[16] and she told Fefe what her ancestor had said. Because Fefe was attracted to Mzusephi, she didn't hesitate to agree. Then Mzusephi told her grandmother she was a lesbian: *"Gogo, uyazi ukuthi mina ngiyinkonkoni yingakho ngizihlalela eGoli ukueze ngingahluphi muntu"* (Grandmother, you know I am a lesbian, that is why I am living in Jo'burg, not to bother anyone). Her grandmother told her that she must respect what the ancestors say and she must marry Fefe.

On Saturday evening Mzusephi came to Fefe's room. She was being polite and telling Fefe about herself and asking questions. Fefe looked out of the window and saw that everybody was drunk on African beer outside so she locked the door and went back to Mzusephi and they made love.

The next morning Mzusephi ran to her grandmother with a happy smile telling her that she respected the word of the

---

15   A ritual to send the ancestors to rest
16   Working space

ancestors but she was not ready for marriage yet. After that Fefe went back home. Mzusephi came to visit but Fefe's family knew her only as Fefe's friend and a grandchild of her trainer.

When Fefe's family found out about her affair with Mzusephi they chased her away from home, saying that what she was doing was sin and it was immoral. They chased her without anything to wear or eat and they burned her working place. Fefe walked to Ladysmith and from there somebody gave her a lift to Johannesburg. When she arrived she had to find where Mzusephi was staying. Finally she found Mzusephi and told her what had happened. Mzusephi let her stay and she bought her new clothes. That is how Fefe knew the ancestors were with her.

One day Mzusephi had a dream that Fefe's ancestors were saying that she must take Fefe back to her roots. She woke Fefe up in the middle of the night and they walked to a nearby park and sat down on the ground under a huge tree. Fefe and Mzusephi looked at each other with tears pouring down their faces and the only words they could say were: "*bogogo nabo mkhulu vulani indlela sizokwazi ukunakhela ikhaya elisha*" (grandmothers and grandfathers, open the way so that we can build you a new home).

On their way back to the flat, Fefe found a plastic bag with something inside it. She picked it up and found it was full of money. She closed it quickly and they ran back to the flat as fast as they could. When they were inside they locked the door and started counting the money. It was two hundred thousand and some rands. Fefe just believed that it was their luck and the money was given to them by their ancestors, so first thing in the morning they took a bus to Piet Retief and bought the land where they now live. Later on they built the house of the ancestors they stay in and the kraal, and they bought cattle and goats. Then they made a ceremony to thank the ancestors and Fefe started her sangoma work. Everything was opened.

Fefe lives according to her ancestors' desires. If they tell her not to go somewhere, she will not go, and they don't like any man next to her. Fefe's ancestor chose Mzusephi for her and told Mzusephi's grandmother that she must marry Fefe, and she did marry Fefe.

Fefe said there are two signs that her ancestors are present. The first is when her right leg starts to tremble. Then she knows that her ancestors are coming into her body. The second sign is when her vagina starts to itch. That is when she knows that her ancestors want sex.

Fefe was a young person. I feel the way she came out to her family was not sensible. Her family was not ready to hear she was a lesbian. She should have checked first and been more careful because she was still young and she needed her family to support her. She needed their resources. I think she made things difficult for herself because she was driven by love. Even though she was not sensible, she was lucky because she was supported by the ancestors all along and they even assisted her by giving her money.

I was surprised that Fefe's trainer allowed her granddaughter to be given as Fefe's ancestral wife. If my ancestors had chosen my trainer's grandchild, my trainer would have felt there was something wrong. In the Zulu culture, you become part of your trainer's family so it was like marrying her sister. I think they should have spoken to the ancestors and said, "No. This cannot happen." It doesn't feel right to me. My trainer taught me how to control my ancestors. We are supposed to learn to control our ancestors. The ancestors work for you if you work with them. You have to learn to control them. I would not allow this to happen.

I have always believed that each life has ups and downs but Fefe's life was so smooth. Her story left me with a lot of questions.

* * *

I heard about Hlengiwe from another sangoma I interviewed in Soweto. When I asked this woman if she could refer me to another lesbian sangoma in her age group, she told me about Hlengiwe. She said Hlengiwe lived in KZN but she would be coming to Diepkloof for a sangoma ceremony, and she invited me to attend the ceremony.

The ceremony started at sunset on a Saturday. When I arrived at the place, Hlengiwe had not yet arrived. I was told she was on her way so I waited for three or four hours and was just about to leave when she arrived with five of her trainees and her partner. I couldn't talk to her at the ceremony because there were so many people there but I asked if I could come and visit her in KZN over the Easter weekend. She agreed and gave me her address.

From the moment I introduced myself to her, Hlengiwe was friendly towards me, even though she came from a different sangoma tradition from mine. There are sangomas who are trained as *Mnguni*, which is the traditional Zulu cultural way, and sangomas who are trained as *Mundawu*. I was trained in the *Mundawu* way. When we greet one another as sangomas, we are greeting the ancestors inside one another. If I see a trainer, I will kneel down and say, "*Thokazani*," which means "blessed one". The sangomas who are trained in *Mnguni* will say "*Makhosi*" when they greet you. It means "the chieftancy". When I greeted Hlengiwe, I knelt down and greeted her in my way. I said, "Thokazani." And she greeted me with "Makhosi.' I learned at that moment that we had been trained differently, although we all embrace the spirit of the ancestors. She had been trained in the Zulu traditional way. With many other *Mnguni* sangomas, if I had greeted them in the *Mundawu* way, they would have rejected me, but Hlengiwe didn't have that in her. There are many sangomas who have been trained in the *Mnguni* way and when you greet them in the *Mundawu* way, they just look at you, they don't greet you back. But with Hlengiwe, I greeted her in my way and she greeted me in her way. She didn't say, "You are not from my way." She was warm and welcoming and I felt that there was a connection between us. I knew immediately that I wanted to see her and spend some time with her.

There are other differences between the *Mnguni* and the *Mundawu*, differences with beliefs, with dancing, with dressing, and some other practices. With *Mnguni*, the focus is on ancestors from your own blood family but with *Mundawu*, your ancestors can be from somebody else's family. They do not have to come from your blood line. Hlengiwe's ancestor was from her husband's family but because she belonged to her husband, his family became her family. Most people prefer to be trained in the traditional way, not the *Mundawu* way.

With *Mundawu*, we have certain steps or stages of dancing. There is dancing while seated first, and then standing and then different stages while standing. But with *Mnguni*, all the dancing is done standing. Then in the dress, with *Mnguni* they put *iSiphandla* around their knees and around their ankles. But with *Mundawu*, you only put *isiphandla* around your wrist on graduation day and that is it.

During training, if you are trained in the *Mundawu* way, you dress in a red cloth with sangoma cloths across your shoulders but you don't smear anything on your body. With *Mnguni* you smear white paste on your body and at a certain stage of the training you smear red paste on your body.

The other thing with *Mnguni* is that they always carry a stick with them. It is called a *phehla*. With *Mundawu*, we have our stick but we don't take the stick with us wherever we go.

After meeting Hlengiwe, I wrote to her and asked her if I could come and spend two days at her place before visiting my uncle over the Easter holidays. She wrote back and said that I should come. She included the cell phone number of one of her trainees and said I should phone when I reached a certain place near where she lived.

I took a taxi from Noord Street in town and travelled for more than six hours to the place where Hlengiwe lives in KZN. On my way, I called the cell number and the trainee put me on to Hlengiwe. She told me where to get off the taxi and said she would send some trainees to meet me. I arrived at nine or ten at night. I could see the trainees waiting for me at the bus stop so I knew where to get off. When I got off the taxi I knelt down and greeted them and they did the same to me.

The trainees took me to Hlengiwe's place. I was not dressed in my sangoma clothes. I was wearing jeans and a T-shirt and jacket and my sneakers. I had my sangoma clothes in my bag. Normally when you visit the house of an older sangoma, you are supposed to wear a traditional cloth as a sign of respect. I didn't do that so when I entered Hlengiwe's house with the trainees she just looked at me and shook her head and without saying anything she went to the next room and came back with a sangoma cloth. She threw it at me. I felt so embarrassed. I caught the cloth and wrapped it around my waist. Then I knelt down and greeted her and she did the same to me.

When I met her, Hlengiwe was a tall, dark, beautiful woman

in her forties, with a slight body. She was dressed in a white doek and traditional cloth and skirt and she was wearing sandals on her feet. Her beads were red and white and she had an *inyoni* tied around her wrists and the *isiphandla* around her legs in the way of the *Mnguni* sangomas. She was wearing a gold ring, identical to the ring her partner, Ntombikhona was wearing. When the two women talked to one another I could see that there was love between them. I could see it in their eyes. The way they live together is quiet and peaceful. They talk quietly and respectfully to one another.

The trainees came with a bowl of water and a cloth and I washed my hands. Then Hlengiwe took me into another room and Ntombikhona brought me some food – pap and beef stew – on a tray. I was very hungry. While I was eating, Hlengiwe asked me a lot of questions about my trainer and my training. She asked me in a polite way. She told me that so many of the young sangomas who train in Johannesburg don't have the ancestral spirit in them but she could see that I have the ancestral spirit in me. She was concerned that so many young sangomas in Soweto seem to be lost. She said they become sangomas for fashion. This is something that concerns me too so I couldn't stop talking and asking her questions. We started talking about training and how people are using training as a business. She reminded me of my trainer when she said, "If somebody comes to you without any money, use your gift to heal that person. Your gift is for healing." Hlengiwe told me that she takes on trainees who cannot pay if they come to her and have a calling. She pointed out one of her trainees who was struggling; her ancestors were pressing down on her and her family was poor so they could not pay for training. Hlengiwe took the girl on as a trainee without worrying about the money.

I told her that in Soweto trainers don't do that. They want money before they take trainees or if they do take them, they won't let them leave until they have paid.

After I had finished eating, she asked me if I wanted something to drink. I said I would have tea. "Are you sure?" she asked. I said, "Well, can I have cold-drink?" She said, "No, no, no. Take off your glasses." I was surprised. I took off my glasses and she looked into my eyes and said, "The man in you wants something stronger than cold-drink." She left the room and came back with a bottle of gin and I poured myself a glass.

Then we went outside to beat the drums. Because I was an elder to the trainees, I had to beat the drums for them so that they could introduce themselves to me. It was Hlengiwe and Ntombikhona and I beating the drums. When people from the area heard the drums they came around to see what was happening. Young boys came and made a fire. It was almost like a ceremony. Hlengiwe sent some of the trainees to get two chickens and they slaughtered them and put them on the fire to braai.

As Hlengiwe and Ntombikhona and I beat the drums, one by one the trainees came and first knelt down in front of Hlengiwe and greeted her and recited their ancestors' names from the very beginning. Each recited his or her whole genealogy in the *Mnguni* way. Then they would come to me and do the same thing and then go to Ntombikhona and do the same thing again. Trainees in the *Mnguni* way must be able to track their ancestry right back to the very beginning of their clan. The ancestors give them this knowledge when they are training. The ancestors show them who they are. They begin to understand where they come from and where they belong and where they are going in life.

I hid something from one of the trainees and waited to see

what she would say. I hid my name and where I was from. She had to come to me and say what it was that I had hidden and then find it. The trainee came down and knelt down in front of me and said, "You have hidden something from me." I said, "Yes, I have. What is it?" She said, "What you have hidden is inside you. You are the great grandfather, Nkunzi, and you come from Thulamashi…" Thulamashi is the name of the place where I go to collect my herbs in Bushbuckridge. I told her. "You have found what I hid for you."

We went to bed around three am. I was feeling very happy when they showed me to the room they had prepared for me. I was given my own hut. The room was very clean with simple furniture: A grass mat on the floor; a single bed; a table and chair; a chest of drawers and a trunk on one side. In the middle of the hut there was a round table with a candle on it. There was no electricity. There was one small window in the hut with no curtain. By the time I went to sleep it was four am. I lay on the bed without blankets because it was very hot. I listened to the sounds of the night which are so different from Meadowlands and I fell asleep feeling very peaceful.

I woke up at about seven am and heard people talking outside. I got up to go outside to the pit toilet, intending to go back to sleep when I returned to my hut because I was still very tired, but when I got back I found a basin and a jug full of hot water. I thought of getting washed but decided to go back to sleep. One of the trainees woke me up by clapping her hands outside the door, "Baba, are you awake?" I called to her to come in. She came in and looked at the water and said, "But you haven't bathed!" I told her I was still sleeping and she should take the water away. I woke up the second time around half past ten. I went outside in my shorts and T-shirt. I found Hlengiwe outside. She said, "You are really a child of Soweto. This is not the time to wake up for a sangoma. Sangomas must wake up early in the morning." I told her I was still tired. She laughed and said all the sangomas from Soweto are like this, they sleep long after sunrise. She asked one of the trainees to bring me more water and I went inside and washed.

After dressing I went outside to the yard. The trainees brought food for me to eat. The others had already eaten breakfast so I ate alone. I was served soft porridge and two slices of bread with peanut butter. When I had finished breakfast, I told Hlengiwe I needed to talk to her privately. She sent the trainees to look after her clients and told them to call her if there was a problem. Then we went to the room where I had first found her and I told her I was doing research about lesbians who are sangomas and I would like to interview her.

First she said, "How did you know about me?" I said, "Someone told me that you are lesbian but you are not out about your lifestyle." She said, "It is true I am not out. I don't see myself as a lesbian. I see myself as a woman who is in love with another woman." I told her that if she gave me her story she would remain anonymous and she made me promise that if she agreed I would make sure her story would not be used in a way that would exploit her. Then she said she wanted to talk to her partner first.

I went outside and walked past the thatched roof huts and into the veld. It is so beautiful in this place. On one side Hlengiwe has planted a huge field of herbs and on the other side there are green fields and trees. I walked in between the herbs and down to a river. There were stones in the river, and small fish. I walked towards the mountains. I heard my ancestors speaking to me from all directions and I went on walking towards the mountains but one of the trainees came running after me and told me not to go there on my own because of the monkeys.

Much later in the day, at around two pm, Hlengiwe's partner, Ntombikhona called me. She said, "You have spoken to Baba. Baba said you are wanting us to tell our story. I don't have a problem as long as you don't mention our names and the place where we live." Then she said, "Someone can see without asking that you are a lesbian, but with us people don't know."

Hlengiwe's story is about growing up in a place where you have to keep your dreams and your thoughts and your feeling inside you. A woman doesn't have a say to a man. A man's word is final. She had to drop out of school before she wanted to and she didn't choose her lover. She had to be chosen.[17]

I interviewed Hlengiwe where she lives in KZN. Her father had 12 wives and there were 20 children in her family. Hlengiwe's mother was the fifth wife and Hlengiwe had two brothers and a younger sister and 16 half brothers and sisters.

Sometimes Hlengiwe wanted to kiss the lips of her half sisters, and touch them, but she couldn't tell anyone because she knew she would be beaten if she talked about that kind of thing in her family.

Her father was strict and traditional. When Hlengiwe was 15 he told her that she had to drop out of school and get married

---

17 Excerpts from this interview first appeared in Nkabinde, N. and Morgan, R. "This has happened since ancient times… it's something you are born with: Ancestral Wives Amongst Same-Sex Sangomas in South Africa". In Morgan, R. and Wieringa, S. *Tommy Boys, Lesbian Men and Ancestral Wives: Female Same-Sex Practices in Africa*. Johannesburg: Jacana Media, 2005. An edited version of the interview by Nkunzi Nkabinde and Ruth Morgan, titled "Unyankwabe: A wife for Zodwa's ancestors," was published in the book: GALZ (ed.) *Unspoken Facts: A History of Homosexualities in Africa*. GALZ: Harare, 2007.

because people from Ndlovu's family were coming to pay lobola for her. She wasn't supposed to disagree with her father's word so she didn't say a thing; she just did what she was told. At the end of the month the Ndlovu family came at the date that was arranged and they brought 18 cattle – two bulls and 16 cows – because Hlengiwe was a virgin.

Two weeks after the lobola was paid, Hlengiwe got married to her husband. Two cows and two goats were slaughtered from Hlengiwe's family's side and from Ndlovu's side they slaughtered two cows and two goats. After this the ancestors from the two families were combined and Hlengiwe had to go and live with her husband.

When she arrived at her husband's place she found that he already had three wives and she was going to be wife number four. There were no children.

Hlengiwe is not a talkative person so she just sat on her own and listened to her thoughts and for three months her husband never came to her room at night. One day in the fourth month he came at night when she was fast asleep. She didn't hear him come in but she woke up when he started to kiss her. She was shivering and her heart was beating so fast because that was the first time she was having a man next to her body. When he started to undress her, a part of Hlengiwe wanted to cry and another part wanted to run away because inside her heart she knew she didn't love this man and she didn't have feelings for him.

During that moment she felt something sitting on top of her stomach and then when her husband tried to be on top of her, she saw it was a snake. He jumped off and said, "There is a snake on top of your stomach!" Hlengiwe sat up straight and the snake just kept on playing around her naked body. Then he said, "Your ancestors are so strong," and he stayed away from her and did not do what he wanted to do. In the morning he woke up and told Hlengiwe he had a dream of his great grandfather telling him not to touch her.

Three years passed and Hlengiwe's husband didn't touch her and then when she was 18 she went to the dam to fetch water one day and saw the face of an old man in the water. She looked behind her, thinking there was somebody standing there but there was no one. When she looked back into the water she saw the old man's face again and he told her to go into the mountains to find his bag of bones which was hidden in a cave. She found herself going to the cave the old man was telling her about and on the way she kept on hearing the voice of the old man saying, "Don't look back."

It was dark when Hlengiwe arrived at the cave. She found an old woman standing outside the cave. The woman said, "I have been waiting for you. Your ancestors told me you were going to come." She took Hlengiwe inside and dressed her in amabhayi and put white muthi on her face and all over her body.

The old woman twisted Hlengiwe's hair and taught her how to grind muthi and how to use it. That is how Hlengiwe started her training and she stayed there for two years.

One day she asked her trainer, "Who is going to bring me food and who is going to tell my husband where I am? She said, "If hunger is what brought you here, you will die, but if it is your ancestors that brought you here, you will live."

The ancestor who called Hlengiwe was the great, great grandfather of her husband, named Mponde. He was a healer at Mzimkulu and his family accused him of witchcraft so he left his family and went to the mountains, where he built his house. Before he died he went back to his family and told his brothers that one of their sons would bring a woman to this family and that woman would be the one to find his bag of bones and his spirit would live through that woman. The brothers were fighting amongst each other so they ignored what he said and after six days they found his dead body in the dam. The family just buried him and forgot about his house and everything he had in there.

Hlengiwe loved the training. She loved the beating of the drums and she liked it when her trainer hid something and she had to search for it. The part she loved most was when her trainer hid four bones inside the dam and she had to swim to find them. She dived into the water and came back with them in her hand.

One day the old woman asked Hlengiwe if she had ever slept with a man. Hlengiwe said she had never slept with a man. Then her trainer asked, "Have you ever slept with a woman?" Hlengiwe said, "How can I sleep with a woman while I am a woman?" Her trainer answered, "You can because I know that inside of you there is a part that wants another woman."

After this Hlengiwe's trainer told her to get undressed and to go and swim naked in the dam for 20 minutes. It was already dark but Hlengiwe did as she was instructed and when she came back naked to the cave her trainer told her to lie down on her back and relax. While she was lying there her trainer came to her naked and knelt beside her and started to caress her and kiss her body all over. Hlengiwe was nervous and her body was trembling. Then her trainer asked, "Mponde, do you want to have a woman or not?" Hlengiwe found herself giving in. She slept with the old woman and started to be free.

After Hlengiwe did not return home for three days, her husband went to her family to tell them that she was missing and they went to all the sangomas in Pietermaritzburg. The sangomas told her family that Hlengiwe was doing the ancestors' work. After two years, Hlengiwe's husband arrived with her father and her uncle. Hlengiwe asked them, "How did you know where I was?" Her uncle told her about his dream. He dreamed of the old man called Mponde Ndlovu, who told him that he had taken Hlengiwe to get his bag. Then he showed her uncle how to get to the cave. Hlengiwe's uncle went to her father and told him about the dream and then her father informed her husband. Hlengiwe's husband told her father that his great grandfather, Mponde Ndlovu, had drowned in a certain dam after leaving his bag of bones in a cave. That is how they knew where to find her.

After this she left her trainer and was welcomed home by her husband and his family. She found that her husband had married another woman while she was away. He told her that Mponde had appeared in his dreams telling him that she belonged to him and he should leave her alone. After this Hlengiwe's husband gave her the house of his ancestor, Mponde, because Hlengiwe is the one with the ancestor's spirit so she has to take what belongs to him. That is how Hlengiwe separated from her husband. Her husband's great grandfather's house is in the mountains, apart from other houses. It is on the opposite side of the mountain from where her husband lives.

After some time of practising as a sangoma, Hlengiwe had a dream of her ancestor telling her about a pregnant woman who would come to her. He said that she should take this woman's child as her own child. The very next day a woman arrived from Egoli, pleading for Hlengiwe to assist her. She was pregnant after being gang raped. She didn't want to have an abortion and she didn't want to keep the child. She said, "It is the child of rape. I don't want to see it."

Hlengiwe sat down with the woman and told her about her dream and she agreed to give Hlengiwe the child after giving birth, so Hlengiwe went to the hospital, to the police, and even to the social workers to sign the papers of agreement. The mother signed the papers with an open heart and Hlengiwe has not seen her since she gave birth to the child.

Meanwhile, Hlengiwe's husband found that he couldn't have children even though he had four wives. He came to Hlengiwe and asked her to plead with the ancestors. He had spent money going to doctors and traditional healers but still there were no children.

Hlengiwe and her husband made a ceremony for the ancestors and slaughtered a goat. A week later her husband came to her and told her that the ancestors had answered and told him in a dream that he must go to the house of Gumede and pay lobola for a girl from that family but the girl would not stay with him, she would stay with Hlengiwe. Hlengiwe didn't disagree. She said, "If that is what the ancestors want, go and find the girl."

Her husband went to look for the family of Gumede because from his dream he knew where to go. Two days later he came back and said that he found the family but the girl, Ntombikhona, is a teacher at the Durban High College so she is not living there. He said the girl's family said they would send for her. A month later the girl came on her own to talk to Hlengiwe's husband. Her husband explained everything to her and then he brought her to meet Hlengiwe and left them alone together.

Hlengiwe took her inside and closed the door and they talked and talked. The girl asked Hlengiwe, "Are you gay?" Hlengiwe didn't understand what she was saying because she had never heard the word "gay", but she looked into the girl's eyes and during that moment there was a vibration that happened to them and Hlengiwe started to have those feelings she had when she was with her trainer in the cave.

The girl asked her, "How can I marry an ancestor who is a man because I do not go with men?" So Hlengiwe explained that the ancestor was in her and she would never have to be with a man. Hlengiwe told her she had never had feelings for a man and she was more attracted to women than to men. Then the girl smiled and said, "Your secret is safe with me. Tell your husband that I said it's okay. He can come and pay the lobola for me." After that Hlengiwe's husband went back to Ntombikhona's place to pay the lobola.

In the month after Ntombikhona joined the family, Hlengiwe's husband's first wife announced that she was pregnant and then the other three wives all fell pregnant as well. That is how Ntombikhona came to stay with Hlengiwe as the wife of Mponde, the great, great grandfather of Hlengiwe's husband.

When I interviewed Hlengiwe, she had been showing her feelings to Ntombikhona for more than 12 years. They sleep together, staying in the same house, and Ntombikhona helps Hlengiwe inside the house and even teaches the *amathwasa*. It is accepted by the community that they live together as Ntombikhona is Hlengiwe's ancestral wife. Their sexual relationship is kept secret. Ntombikhona has learned to beat the drums and the children love her as a mother, although they don't know that Ntombikhona and Hlengiwe are lovers. It is a secret.

Hlengiwe's ancestors influenced her because they didn't allow her to enjoy her young days and they made her an isolated person. They allowed her to be married to a man and again they brought a woman for her. They let her have a secret life with this woman and she is in love with this woman. With the man, she has respect but no feelings but he looks after her and he cares for her very much.

Normally Hlengiwe's ancestor, Mponde, doesn't influence her to be a man. She said she is 100 per cent a lady who doesn't like to be with a man and she and Ntombikhona are just two women loving each other. But when Mponde's spirit is around, she becomes like a man. She will want Ntombikhona to dress her and to help her with things like mixing muthi. Sometimes when it is time for Mponde to come, when Hlengiwe dances or when she is at the *enamo*,[18] she becomes like a man. Her voice changes and her body becomes tough like a man's body. If she is not in Mponde's spirit, Hlengiwe is a lady who loves her womanhood and who loves the woman next to her.

After Hlengiwe had been talking for some time, she said something very strange: "Look at me. Is there something different between me and you, because I don't see it." She said, "Me and you are the same." I was trying to understand what she was saying and after a while I realized that Hlengiwe feels connected to everything and everyone. It is like there is a huge space inside her, big enough for the whole world. The whole world is in her and she is in the whole world. It was amazing for me to think about the things she said to me. The information she gave me was amazing and the way she spoke to me was as if she was making a documentary. I felt that she was saying, "Hold on to this thing and if I die use it well." It was as if she was giving her last will and testament to me.

Hlengiwe spoke to me as if I was her equal. Normally in African culture, you don't question an older woman the way I questioned her but she made me an equal. Hlengiwe is a humble

---

18 The place where she prepares her remedies

person and she is down to earth. Every question I asked her, she answered directly. When I asked her, "How did you feel when you had your first sexual experience with your trainer?" She said, "I was very scared. I was very nervous." She spoke honestly. She answered directly and her answers were to the point. She looked into my eyes when she spoke to me. I loved that.

I was impressed by Hlengiwe's humility and her obedience. From the start, when her father took her out of school to marry her off, she didn't refuse. I would have questioned and argued but she obeyed. When her husband paid lobola for her and she went to stay with his family, she didn't resist. She went with him. And when her husband wanted to have sex with her, she didn't fight. She just agreed and obeyed. And even when the ancestor appeared in the form of a snake on top of her, she didn't scream. That was amazing for me. When I asked her about it she said, "I thought it was my husband but my husband was standing next to the door. Then when I looked at my belly I saw this small snake, and it was playing all over my body. I was not scared. I found myself smiling at the snake and asking myself, where did it come from? Did it come from inside me? My husband was standing there and he was scared. His face was full of fear. But I was not afraid."

The other part of Hlengiwe's story that I loved is when Ntombikhona came to stay with her. Hlengiwe did not choose Ntombikhona. She just accepted that this was the right partner for her. She had no questions. Everything for Hlengiwe was paved. Her ancestors paved the way for her.

Even though Hlengiwe's relationship with her husband was like a sister and brother relationship, she respected him and she obeyed him as her husband. I asked her, "Do you love your husband?" She said, "What is love?" She explained that she loves her husband for helping her to see the path and for supporting her on the path, but her real love is for Ntombikhona.

I was supposed to stay at Hlengiwe's place for two days but I ended up staying for three days. There is such a peaceful atmosphere around Hlengiwe and Ntombikhona. Everyone is happy there. Even the trainees will say, "Baba is always happy so we are always happy." There was warmth at Hlengiwe's place. It did not feel strange for me. It felt like home.

After my interview with Hlengiwe, we fasted for two days and only drank water. She made me stop smoking my cigarettes. We stayed in a room together and prayed and communicated with our ancestors. We wore white cloths around our waists and our breasts were not covered. We were preparing to go and find healing herbs and plants in the mountains. If you are pure when you go and find the herbs, you are protected. If not, you can die or be crippled, or the herbs will not allow you to find them and you will be lost forever in the bush.

Hlengiwe taught me to be humble in front of the plants. She taught me to know the difference between the plants and to know how to communicate with the plants if I am in the bush. I learned how to listen to the sounds of the plants. Hlengiwe told me, "The plants are talking you. They are communicating with you. Even the water itself is communicating with you. Listen!"

After we had fasted for two days, Hlengiwe took me into the bush. She taught me what to wear and what to do. She gave me a panga and an axe and I took my sangoma bag to put the herbs in. An old man and four trainees went with us. There were about seven of us altogether. Before we entered the bush, we took off our shoes and knelt down. Hlengiwe burned *Impepho*, the herb that is burned before communicating with the ancestors, and she told the ancestors we had come to look for herbs and they should guide us and if there is evil or danger, clear the way for us. There was a breeze and I could hear the voice of my mom telling me to come this side or that side.

The friendship I built with Hlengiwe has kept me going through difficult times. If I have a dream I will write to her and she will reply and tell me what it means. If I have a difficult client, I will write to Hlengiwe and she will tell me what to do. Because Hlengiwe did not finish school, she dictates the letters and Ntombikhona writes them.

There are many herbs and plants that Hlengiwe has shown me. One example is using *Mphunyuka*, which comes from a bush with small leaves and white flowers. I never believed in it but after I phoned Hlengiwe about some trouble a cousin of mine was having, she told me to use it. There were some men who wanted to kill my cousin and Hlengiwe told me to take the Mphunyuka leaves and mix them with some other herbs. I took some of the herbs and told my cousin to put them in his bath and to smear the herbs on his chest and put them in his shoes. As he walked out, the people who were looking for him were waiting for him but they didn't recognise him. They asked, "Where can we find Bongani?" He said, "I don't know," and walked away down the road. After that I trusted that herb but my cousin used to come to me whenever he was in trouble until he became too much and I told him to go away. I told him, "If you go and start robbing people and then come to me, I won't be helping you."

These days Hlengiwe also has a cell phone, although she is still learning how to use it, and sometimes I call her if I need advice.

The two people who made the most impact on me were Bongiwe and Hlengiwe. Bongiwe taught me how to live a free life as a lesbian and a sangoma in Johannesburg. Hlengiwe has helped me to become a more powerful healer.

The interviewing work for GALA gave me a new understanding of my identity, my culture, and my place in my country.

CHAPTER EIGHT

The Ancestors Don't Mind

WHEN MY TRAINER and my elders saw me at sangoma ceremonies with my girlfriends and heard about my relationships with women, they were not happy. My trainer said, "This is not allowed." I told her, "If it is not allowed, why did you accept me?" She said, "You are supposed to change." I said, "Can I change feelings? Can I change the colour of my blood? Can you change my blood from red to green?"

I went to see a famous sangoma who passed away some time later. His name was Nkomo Yahlaba. I explained that there are gay and lesbian sangomas who are afraid to come out. I told him I would never hide my feelings but the elders said I should live my sex life secretly because lesbians are not part of African life. I said I cannot live my life secretly. I want to be open. Secrecy is not in me. He said, "What they are telling you is a lie."

I told my trainer what Nkomo Yahlaba said. I told her being a lesbian was as African as being a straight person. She refused to understand or to compromise and the elders were behind her, backing her up. I told them they could take away my training, my certificate, everything! But they would not be able to take away my ancestors and my pride.

My trainer called me to a meeting at her house. When I arrived

I found 20 elders, most of them men, waiting for me. They sat in a circle in a room in my trainer's house, some of them on chairs and others on grass mats. They told me that they knew about my same-sex relationships and all they were asking was that I hide my sexuality. I told them I would never hide it because it is like a scar: if I hide it, it won't be healed. For the scar to be healed you have to wrap it then wash it and unwrap it, and then it will be dry.

They reprimanded me for talking too much and for answering back. I said, "If I don't talk, who is going to talk for me?" I asked a lot of questions and I challenged them, accusing some of them of proposing to me and telling them that their children also wanted me. "You have got your sex life and I have got mine," I told them. I told them my mother had accepted me, so I didn't need their approval.

Eventually they told me to go outside so they could talk about what I had said. They said I should wait until they called me. I left the room and went home. I never went back. My trainer phoned me on my cell phone. She was angry and she shouted at me: "Where are you? We told you to wait." I said, "I am not waiting outside while you discuss me. You are not my parents." She was angry with me and I was angry with her. There was no more trust and there was tension between us.

I was so angry after this that I decided I wanted to go public as soon as possible. At the same time I wanted to help other same-sex sangomas who were being judged and oppressed by the sangoma community.

While I was doing the research for GALA I interviewed a gay sangoma named Grace. I went to see him and told him what had happened. He was so furious that he phoned the elders one by one and told them what he thought of them. Grace introduced me to other same-sex sangomas who lived some distance away from Soweto, in the Vaal area. He took me to their ceremonies in Randfontein and Sebokeng. I felt at home with other gay and lesbian sangomas and I decided I was not going to heterosexual sangoma ceremonies anymore. My trainer called me to come to ceremonies and I told her, "I am a lesbian. You said you don't want people like me."

After a while, Grace and I started to talk about forming an organisation for same-sex sangomas. Sangomas are supposed to work together. They need to share their knowledge and support and protect one another and to combine their herbs and treatments. Grace had a ceremony and we invited same-sex sangomas. After dancing together and calling on our ancestors to guide us, we sat down and discussed the idea of forming an organisation. There was support for the idea. We started the Sangomas Coming Out group with 10 gay and lesbian sangomas from all over the Gauteng province.

My opportunity to go public came when I became involved with the GALA Queer Tour. I was one of the tour guides trained by GALA when the tour was updated in 2002. The GALA Queer Tour takes people from the suburbs of Johannesburg to the inner city areas of Braamfontein and Hillbrow before ending up in Soweto. The tour shows that black and white gays and lesbians have been around since the very beginning.

No one talks about homosexuality in my culture. People always hide it. They say it doesn't exist in our history. I saw a film about a girl being guided by one of the elders and it shows Zulu life. It shows how in traditional society a Zulu girl is always amongst other girls in all the important phases of life. There was always that closeness between girls and there were always girls who wanted to extend those feelings but they couldn't, so they were hidden away.

How can people know when it was hidden away? No one wants to talk about it but such things were always there. One of the women I interviewed in KwaZulu-Natal said the problem in rural areas is that people have to hide their feelings and everything in them because of stigma. She said being next to a woman is one thing that was definitely there because you will find that from ancient times women were left there alone and men went to do hunting. When women were together in a room and the kids were outside playing, they would start chatting and then when they looked at each other there would be that closeness and they would feel there was something more they wanted to do together. But because they were afraid, they couldn't explore their feelings. I believe there was always love between women in my culture but no one wants to talk about it.

If you go back to Shaka's day, you will find it there.[1] It was there. They hide it. It is like when you play hide and seek when you are a kid. You go behind the wall and that is where you kiss. You start to touch, or some of the girls were masturbating. It was there but they don't want to talk about it. It definitely goes back to Shaka's day.

When it comes to the Soweto part of the tour, one of the GALA guides talks about the history of Soweto, explaining that Soweto was built by the apartheid authorities to be a dormitory town for black labour but it has turned into a city.

When the bus gets to Meadowlands the tourists first hear the history of how people were forcibly removed from Sophiatown and made to live in Meadowlands. Then they are told about the history of the single sex hostels which were built for migrant

---

1 Shaka, the famous Zulu king of the nineteenth century, used to encourage his soldiers to engage in *hlobongo*, thigh sex, with one another.

labourers who came to Egoli to work on the gold mines. There are also many stories about the homosexuality that was happening in those hostels. Men in the hostels used to have same-sex relationships with other men. I have been told that in the mines the traditional practice of *mteto*[2] was common. Meanwhile, the wives of these men who were left alone in the rural areas used to get involved in same-sex relationships with one another because there were no men around.

There is a story about two elderly men who used to rent a room in the hostel so they could continue with their gay relationship in secret. It was difficult for these men in the 1960s and 1970s to live a public or full time gay life so they each had wives and children. During the week they stayed with their families and on Fridays they would go to that rented room in the hostel in Meadowlands and stay together there for Friday night, Saturday, Sunday, until on Monday they went back to being husband and father again. These men are still alive and although they are not together anymore, they still keep in contact. Both of them are old men now and they live with their wives and families separately in Soweto.

The gay sub-culture that is happening in the township is also discussed on the tour. Most gay and lesbian couples imitate straight relationships, with one playing the masculine part and one playing the feminine part. This came up in the research I did for GALA. For example, when I interviewed Mashudu she said, "Ntuthuko… was my 'man'. She was everything I ever wanted from past relationships. She was the only one who knew how to treat me like a lady. I was her lady and she was my man."

Until our society changes, gay relationships will follow suit.

---

2   A same-sex marriage ceremony in which novices are "married" to veterans

Some straight men beat their wives and some butch lesbians do the same. So there is that kind of idea that being butch means being in control, like in patriarchy where men are responsible for things. There are so many women who think that if you don't give them a *klap*, you don't love them. Most women – straight and lesbian women – are like this. It comes from ancient times. Some women still say that if their husbands show them love they have to beat them. That is how a husband shows that he still cares. Lesbians carry this into their relationships. There is a lot of beating with lesbians too. There is one girl I know who is so abusive. She beats her partners. Some stay and some run away.

There has always been violence in straight relationships and in same-sex relationships. I did that in the past. I raised my hand to my partner. It was the first time I did something like that in my life and I apologised afterwards. I have never done it again. I was angry. It was me who was angry, not my ancestor. I was just so angry. I was jealous. My partner has a beautiful body and she knows that I am jealous. I don't like it if she spends too much time speaking to people she knows when we go out together, like when we go to the mall. I prefer to spend time indoors when I am in Meadowlands. In KZN, everything is different.

When it comes to gay men the same thing happens; you have one that is feminine and one that is masculine and the interesting part about that is that the masculine man is always a straight man. Even though in the township everyone knows this man is sleeping with other men, his sexual identity doesn't change. He remains a straight man. And then among the gay men there are other people who we call the "fifty-fifties". They don't mind either role. It all depends on the relationship they find themselves in.

Some lesbians and gays feel we don't need to copy everything that straight couples are doing. Sometimes there is no particular role or sometimes they might take a particular role for a particular relationships and the next relationship they take a completely different role. We call it "mixed masala". These days, couples who want to do the role playing might feel stigmatised by more progressive attitudes. The progressives say, "Why copy? Why can't we be just women who love women or just men who love men without role playing?"

One sangoma I interviewed said, "Before I used to be butch and then I changed. I realized being butch and refusing to cook and clean was wrong. I decided to be in between and I was comfortable with that. So presently I am not butch or feminine. I am in between. I do wear a skirt but underneath I wear tights. I do that so I do not have a problem when the ancestors want trousers."

After the discussion on sub-culture, the tour stops at Ipelegeng where Simon Nkoli started the Township Aids Project. Simon was the first black person to come out as gay and the first black person to come out as HIV-positive. He came out while he was still in prison in connection with the Delmas Treason Trial. When he was released from prison in 1989, Simon founded a gay and lesbian organisation called GLOW (Gay and Lesbian Organisation of the Witwatersrand). It was the first organisation for black gays and lesbians. Simon's message was that gays and lesbians were African and they were Christian. He had a big impact on other gays and lesbians, encouraging people to come out in spite of the stigma. Simon was like a father to some young people. I heard about him from a friend and he became a brother to me.

I met Simon's partner, Roy Shepherd, at the library in Market Street in town. I used to go there because they had a small selection of gay and lesbian books. I started visiting the library from the age of 13 or 14 but I was much older when I met Roy. I met him after Simon died in 1998. I read books by Mary Renault like *The King Must Die*, and I read *The Well of Loneliness* by Radclyffe Hall and *Oranges Are Not the Only Fruit*, by Jeanette Winterson. I also remember books by Pat Califia. It took me a long time to read these books because the English was a challenge for me but I found people to help me, explain to me and discuss with me.

Even though gay men like Simon, Edwin Cameron, Peter Bussey and Zackie Achmat have always been in the forefront of the fight against HIV, the interventions by government and NGOs are always directed at straight people. At the Chris Hani Baragwanath Hospital in Soweto, the largest hospital in the southern hemisphere, HIV research and antiretroviral drug trials have been done. HIV is widespread in Soweto and nobody is excluded from the numbers who are coping with the virus or dying from it, but the official statistics are based on research with pregnant women. That means the whole gay population is excluded from the research.

The person in charge of the Soweto HIV/AIDS Counselling Association (SOWACA) is a drag queen named Thulani. He is forever in drag and he doesn't get attacked and there is no violence against him. He is following in the steps of Simon in the township. He does all kinds of HIV work in the township. People respect him for the work he does for them so he is not a target for prejudice or violence.

When the tour passes the Hector Pieterson Museum, the question is, "Why is the museum relevant for gay people?" The answer is that the 1976 rebellion was not only about Afrikaans being the medium of instruction, it was also a generational rebellion because young people were tired of the way things had always been done. They looked at the elders and they thought they were too conventional and too slow and they said, "You know what, we are tired of this." And out of that rebellion there were gay men. That generation gave birth to leaders like Simon, who started out as political activists and then they became gay activists as well.

During the tour, there are questions about belief systems. Not all gays and lesbians are Christians. From here the tourists come to my house to see what it means to work with ancestors and African traditional beliefs.

I explain about my life and what it means to be a lesbian sangoma, the challenges as well as the advantages. I tell them, "In the townships people believe that sangomas have supernatural powers so they think twice before they do anything. They are afraid of the consequences. People are especially scared of witchcraft."

Outside my house I explain about the tree that is wrapped in a sangoma cloth. This is the place that is known as *Epandeni*. The tree is there for the ancestors from outside, from the fields. When you go to the mountains to pray you are calling these ancestors. They are the ones who know everything that is happening outside and they are the ones who report to me fast when I am inside the house or consulting room that someone is coming from outside. They protect me and that is why they are situated outside. Each and every year when they get cold they tell me the colour of the cloth they want me to get for them to keep them warm and I do this. When I put the cloth here for them, I do a ceremony with *Ikhamba*.

Afterwards I ask the people to take off their shoes out of respect for my ancestors before entering my consulting room.

Then they sit on the floor and I explain that the ancestors from the river stay inside the consulting room. They are used to staying under the water. Their place is called *Umnthundu*.

Then I show them my bones and explain how they are used. First I call my ancestors and then I throw the bones and they tell me what's wrong with the person who comes to see me. The same with my herbs. Before giving somebody herbs to take, I wait for instructions from my ancestors who tell me which herbs to use for different illnesses.

The Queer Tour is a success and many people from the media have interviewed me. When the elders read about me in the newspapers and saw my picture there, my trainer called me. She was very upset and angry. "How can you do this?" she said. And I replied, "I want the world to know that there are lesbian sangomas." I asked her, "Next time you find a child who is a lesbian who is suffering because of her ancestors and she wants to do the training, what are you going to do? Are you going to lie to her or chase her away?"

A few days later she called me and asked me to come and see her. When I arrived at her house I felt sadness in me because I had gone from being mentally disturbed to being a healer in this place and there were many memories. Now it seemed like there were only problems between me and my trainer. I sat down opposite her the way I had many times before. She looked straight at me and said, "I am sorry. I didn't know. It's the first time I have had to deal with this." I could see that she was trying her best to accept me.

After the meeting with my trainer, the elders contacted Grace. They had heard about our organisation and they wanted to meet us. Grace persuaded me to go with him because he said we are all sangomas and we all do the same work. When we arrived there I found the same elders who had ordered me to keep my sexuality a secret. They had also changed their attitude and they apologised for judging me. They said gay and lesbian people who are called to be sangomas must feel accepted. I could see it was hard for them to say these things because there was still this belief in them that being gay or lesbian is not African.

I realized that our organisation must continue because there will always be this tension in the sangoma community. Today there are 40 same-sex sangomas aged between 18 and 34 in my organisation. When we get together we talk about the herbs we are using and what we are using them for and when we go to ceremonies we don't feel isolated. I wanted people to feel connected, not rejected. In this we have been successful.

CHAPTER NINE

Doing Things Differently

ONE DAY I WAS AT THE GALA offices when somebody called Ruth and asked if she knew anyone who was interested in becoming a tour guide at Constitution Hill. I was sitting there and Ruth asked me if I was interested. I was. Once again, GALA opened up a door for me on one side and my ancestors were organising things for me on the other side.

I was trained by Jacqui du Plessis from Empower Ed. There were 16 of us attending classes every day for seven months. I learned about how to be a tour guide and my eyes were opened to a whole lot of my history that I didn't know about before.

During the training I was inspired by the Constitutional Court judges, especially Judge Albie Sachs. I have always respected him because of his attitude to gays and lesbians. In 1962, a man called Cecil Williams was arrested with past president Nelson Mandela in KZN. Cecil Williams was an important person in the early days of the anti-apartheid struggle and he was also well known for his work in the theatre. Everyone knew he was gay but he lived his gay life and his political life separately. A film[1] that was made about him was

---

1 *The Man Who Drove Mandela.* Documentary film researched and written by Mark Gevisser and produced by Greta Schiller. 1998

written by Mark Gevisser, who was one of the people who helped to design GALA's Queer Tour. When Mark was doing the research for the film, Albie Sachs told him, "If you want to understand why the African National Congress is so tolerant of gay people, look to Comrade Cecil Williams."

When Albie Sachs explained the symbolism of the new court building I felt excited about being a lesbian in South Africa because of our progressive Constitution. On the other side, I was very disturbed and shocked to hear about the history of the Old Fort prison and the Women's Jail.

The women's prison has been modernised in parts, and some of the cells have been demolished, but when you go to the male section you still have the feeling that this is a prison. There is a feeling of the history that is very strong in the men's prison.

The Women's Jail was built in 1909. Black and white women were held in different sections. The communal cells for black women were designed for 50 women prisoners but when the prison was overcrowded there were up to 250 women prisoners in the cells.

One of the famous women in the Women's Jail was Winnie Madikizela Mandela. She was in the isolation cells and she took a stand for women. When she was released, Winnie walked into the middle of the main section of the prison and said, "I am standing here because I am fighting for the rights of women." After that, women were allowed to walk into that space.

I love Winnie Mandela. I think she is a woman of courage, a brave woman, and a woman of her word. None of the bad things that people have said about her have been proven. I don't think Winnie did anything violent to anybody. I don't think she is capable of any violence. If people say bad things about Winnie I tell them, "We all have our own scandals. No one is a saint in this world."

I grew up with a mixture of stories about Number 4. My Uncle Ray was in prison there before he went into exile but I only found out about that when I was much older. As a younger child I remember how my sisters and I used to laugh at another uncle because he drank too much. We used to tease him until he lost his temper and he would say, "I am going to *bliksem* you and I am going to go back to Number 4!" Often he disappeared unexpectedly and we thought he had gone to Number 4 whenever he disappeared. We thought Number 4 was a kind of a hotel where he disappeared to. It was only when I was working at Constitution Hill that I found out about Number 4 and some part of me felt bad thinking of my uncle in this place and how unbearable it must have been.

I was not prepared for the sad memories of ex-prisoners I met during the training. Some of them were old and sick and uneducated and I felt pity for them. After meeting them I understood in a new way how apartheid pressed down on the lives of my mother and father and my ancestors.

One of the ex-prisoners I met was a woman called Patricia Alarm who was put in prison for not having a pass. She became a gang boss in the Women's Jail. The gang bosses had sex with other women, they called it *"snaganaga."* Her life inside was unbearable. She was a fighter like me and once when she had a fight with the wardresses, they called the male warders from The Fort to come and help them. The male warders beat her up and destroyed her arm. I was touched by her story. Since she had her hand damaged in prison she couldn't find work because she is a domestic worker and she can't work with one hand. She survives on grant money.

Another ex-prisoner who made an impression on me was called "Yvonne." She was imprisoned for just holding hands with a white person. She was arrested under the Immorality Act.

Then there was Jack Mabaso who said he did crime because he was hungry. Once when he was in Rissik Street in town he saw a white lady drop her purse so he kneeled down to pick it up for her. The lady screamed and screamed until the police came and she told them, "This black boy wants to rob me." But it wasn't true. All he wanted to do was to help her. She had him arrested and he was taken to The Fort. After that he became angry towards white people and he started a life of crime. He told me the life in the Old Fort was terrible. I know myself from working at Con. Hill what a cold place it is, especially in winter. He told me he would be locked in the isolation cells without a blanket and when he came out of there, because he was used to being alone, it was too much for him to go into a communal cell with other prisoners. He felt like he was losing his mind.

I noticed that many of the prisoners turned into alcoholics because of their pain. This disturbed me very much. I think I would have been one of the people who was shot and killed for fighting back. Many stories that happened in Constitution Hill are not told. I heard a story of a young boy who was raped by one of the gang bosses and he was so angry that he smashed the head of the gang boss against the toilet seat and killed him. There was so much violence there. I can feel it still in my spirit.

I love working at Constitution Hill because it holds the past and the future but I wouldn't have survived if I was in prison there. Working at Constitution Hill means working with a mixture of feelings every day. It is a place where there is pain and also hope, and it is a place where there is forgiveness but also scars that will always be there. This is because on the one side there is sadness about our history and on the other side there is the Constitutional Court which is a place of hope. When I feel this hope in me, I feel that I have everything I need inside me to make a better world. I think my ancestors organised my job as a tour guide at Constitution Hill because it is a place where the old and the new come together in a different way. It makes me think of what my ancestor, Nkunzi said, "After I die, one of the grandchildren will take my name and follow after me and do things in a different way."

The other thing about working at Constitution Hill is that it is a place where the spirit world bumps into every day life. In African culture, when someone dies, the elders have to go to the area where that person has died and take the spirit away. People were beaten up and killed in these prisons, especially in the Old Fort. They died here and their spirits have never been taken away. There are lots of spirits still here. I can feel them.

Before they closed the Old Fort for renovations I would take visitors to the white men's cells and then to the Mandela section because there is such a big difference between them. Our past was very bad and there was terrible discrimination. It was as if the black person was worth nothing and neither was his life or his family worth anything.

There is an exhibition inside the Mandela cell which is about the life history of Mandela. It shows some of the things he used in prison and on Robben Island and gives a little background about him before he was imprisoned. Before he was sent to Robben Island, Mandela was held at the awaiting trial block before being transferred to the Old Fort. This was in 1962. The awaiting trial block was built in 1928 and demolished in 2003. Mandela was held there for two to three weeks, then they said they were going to move him to the Old Fort. He asked them, "Why are you taking me there when it is for white prisoners only and I am black."

They told him it was because of his status as a lawyer. They told him they would provide him with a better room and he would have his bed and his books. And if he got sick, there would be access to medical care. But Mandela and the members of the ANC never believed that. They believed that the reason they moved Mandela to the Old Fort was to watch him closely and if he tried to escape it would be easy for them to shoot and kill. Also as one black man between whites it was easy to keep track of him. If he stayed in the awaiting trial block he was just one black man among many.

The exhibition in the Mandela cell includes a collection of letters he wrote while he was on Robben Island and there is a video clip showing Mandela when he was on Robben Island.

After this, visitors are taken to Number 4. This is where sentenced black men were held in communal cells. I show them the cells and how life was in the cells and how prisoners were treated inside there. White prisoners were given a mattress, a pillow, three blankets, four sheets, two pillowcases and a bedspread. The non-white prisoners were given two sleeping mats and a blanket. There were gangsters in the prison who stole the blankets of incoming prisoners in order to create a comfortable layer, which looks like a mattress, for their leaders. So you find that the leaders would sleep on one side. Those who were close to the leaders would sleep to one side, close to them. And the rest of the gang members would sleep at the back. If you were not a member of the gang or if you were a newcomer, you would sleep next to the toilet. The room was designed for 30 prisoners but it was overcrowded and had up to 60 prisoners until the prison was closed down in 1983.

The main section of Number 4 is the where I feel most moved. In Number 4, for me as a sangoma, I feel in me – in my body, in my shoulders – that there is a person who wants to talk but I don't know how to communicate. There is a presence definitely. It is there.

Then visitors see the food area and there is an exhibition of panels showing the kind of food that was given to the prisoners. The white men were given better food than coloured and Asian men and coloured and Asian men had better food than African men. Whites, coloured and Asian men were given bread but Africans never had bread. Whites had a menu and they could choose. It was not the same food every day. Blacks were given rotten fish or mieliemeal. At Christmas white prisoners were given pudding or cake. Non-whites were given one pinch of coffee or tea with one pinch of sugar.

After this, I take them to the area called the *Lekgotla* space: the place for gathering together. In that area, prisoners took their food and ate it. It was disgusting because the area is next to the toilets and the toilets were the squatting toilets; they didn't have toilet seats. The prisoners had to sit on the gravel. There were no chairs. The area became known as "Lekgotla" after political prisoners saw a humiliating picture of the men doing the "Tauza", taken by Bob Gosani who was working for *Drum Magazine.* Some of the prisoners were hired to go and do manual work outside. When they came back they had to be searched. They said the prisoners normally hid money and razor blades in their anuses. That is why they performed Tauza on them. Tauza means you have to be stripped naked, jump around, clap your hands, bend down and have your anus searched.

I heard that white gay men who lived in a block of flats overlooking the courtyard where Tauza happened used to watch from the balcony of their flat. They were part of a completely different world.

Doing Things Differently

In African culture it is not acceptable for an older man to get undressed in the presence of a younger man but in prison men were forced to strip in front of everyone. When the political prisoners saw the Tauza picture, they were so furious they fought with warders and said there would be no more Tauza because it is not allowed in our culture. Eventually political prisoners won the struggle. They were never subjected to Tauza. It was only done to common law prisoners.

After talking about Tauza, I take them to the shower space. The prisoners took showers outside and never had hot water. The prisoners had to spend 30 minutes in the shower and they were only allowed to take one shower a week. They never had hot water. It was always cold water. Meanwhile, white prisoners at the Old Fort were allowed to take a shower seven days of the week and they had hot and cold water.

After that, I take the visitors to the room where there are some sculptures made by the prisoners using their blankets. There is a sculpture of a tank and a sculpture of flowers in a flower pot. These are things created by the prisoners with their own hands using their blankets.

Then I take them to the "power and punishment" cell where you find the instruments they used to punish prisoners, like sjamboks, chains, keys to lock the doors, all those things. If prisoners were sentenced to corporal punishment they would have to stand here and they would maybe be flogged on the back with 30 or 40 lashes. Afterwards they would be taken to the isolation cells. Prisoners had to spend 23 hours without food or water.

They would be given two buckets if they spent the week there, one filled with water and the other with half water. The full water was for drinking and the half water was where they had to "do their business". Because it was always dark in the isolation cells, the prisoners had to be careful which bucket they used. If you used the wrong bucket you would spend the whole night without water unless you drank the water you had messed in.

After this I take the visitors to the room where prisoners were taken if they had to do an extra punishment. Here prisoners were hosed down in either summer or winter and they were locked in there for 24 hours.

Next we go to the Constitutional Court. I explain that the reason why the court is here is to try and heal the injustices of the past. The court is built where the old awaiting trial block used to be. When they demolished the awaiting trial block they built four staircases. Two are outside and two have been incorporated into the court building as a reminder of the past. In each staircase there is a glass tower showing the rise of the future South Africa.

Some of the bricks from the awaiting trial block were used to build the walls of the court. The way the court is designed is that it is like a tree, meaning justice under a tree. Why? In African culture, our elders normally go and discuss a case under a tree. The difference here is that in African culture only men were allowed to sit under the tree, not women. But now we say all of us can come and sit in the Constitutional Court, no matter what the colour of your skin or your gender.

Before I take visitors inside the court I explain about the writing on the outside wall of the court. I tell them, in South Africa we have 11 official languages. That is why we have "Constitutional Court" written in 11 languages in different colours. Then, in the concrete on top of the court the judges have written in their own handwriting the words, *human dignity, equality* and *freedom* in all the 11 official languages.

The wooden door which was designed in KZN has 27

numbers which are the basic themes of our Bill of Rights, including sign language. If you touch the handle of the door you will feel the Braille writing telling us that our Constitution does not exclude anyone. The South African Constitution was the first constitution in the world to make it a crime to discriminate against people because of their sexual orientation, and South Africa was the first African country to introduce a law which allows same-sex marriages. The Civil Union Act of 2006 gives gay and lesbian people the same rights as straight people.

In the foyer of the court I point out that the chandelier has leaves made out of wire. They are like the leaves of a tree. The pillars in the corners of the foyer represent the trunk of a tree. The pillars are not standing straight so it looks as if the court is not balanced. This is because the tree includes different shapes and different sizes, the same as the pillars of the court. Then I take visitors inside the chamber and they see how the court has been designed like a tree and they see the table for the judges. We have 11 judges, they are called Justices, and so there are 11 chairs behind a long table that is covered in ox skin. The Chief Justice, Justice Pius Lange, always sits in the middle and his deputy, Dikgang Moseneke, sits on his right side. The other justices rotate and they can sit anywhere they like.

After this I show them the table for the judges' assistants and the area for the advocates. Up above are the area for the public gallery, the area for the media, and the area for the translators and transcribers of our 11 official languages.

The glass panel in the court is telling us about transparency. In the past, information was hidden away and nobody could find out what was really going on but in the democratic South Africa we have the right to ask for information and to be given it. Then I tell visitors about the bricks. Why did they use the old bricks from the awaiting trial block in the court? It is to tell us younger generation that we should not dwell on the past but from the mistakes of the past we should try and build a better future.

Finally, I explain to visitors that the Constitutional Court is the highest court in the land and it deals only with constitutional matters. I tell them that if someone violates my rights, my case will come to the Constitutional Court.

Being near the court and talking about it to visitors from all over the world has given me more confidence in myself. I know that as a Zulu lesbian I have rights and I deserve to be protected.

My work as a tour guide at Constitutional Hill also keeps me connected with organisations fighting for gay and lesbian rights that have offices there, and other human rights groups that use the facilities for meetings.

CHAPTER 10

Hate Crimes

I MET SIZAKELE SIGASA at a party in Dube. She was tall and slim and she wore jeans and boots. I was attracted to her. She was talkative and we started talking and then we started dating. Our relationship lasted for seven or eight months. I had dreads at that time, long dreads, but I wanted to shave my head. She didn't like me to be a tomboy. She wanted to bring out the feminine side in me. She didn't like the masculine side of me. I told her, "That is me. It will never change." It became a problem in our relationship. There were other problems, too. We liked different things. I liked to stay at home and watch TV. Sizakele liked going to clubs. After my calling I couldn't stand clubs because the beat of the sangoma drums was so different from the beat of the music they play in clubs. I was forbidden to go there by Nkunzi until I graduated as a sangoma and then I started going again from time to time, but I would rather do something else. The music makes me feel sick. Even travelling to work in a taxi is hard for me when they play loud music. Sometimes it is so unbearable that I ask the taxi to stop and I get off. The noise disturbs the peace inside me and I can't hear what the ancestors are saying to me. I prefer to travel by train.

In the end Sizakele and I agreed that it wasn't going to work for us. We remained friends and used to bump into one another from time to time. I couldn't believe it when somebody called me to say she was dead. Who? Where? How? Piece by piece the horrible story of Sizakele's death spread across Johannesburg and made headlines in all the newspapers in Johannesburg.

Sizakele and her partner, Salome Masooa, were last seen at the opening of Breeze, a gay and lesbian shebeen in Orlando in Soweto. Apparently Sizakele and another lesbian were fighting over Salome. Friends stepped in to stop the fight and just before midnight Sizakele and Salome left, with Sizakele promising to be back later. Sizakele had her own car and lived in a rented house in Meadowlands. She never returned. Her friends kept on ringing her cell but there was no reply. The next morning the news of her death spread like fire. Sizakele and Salome were found by a man who was jogging past a vacant plot. Both had been raped and brutally murdered. Sizakele was found with her hands tied together with her underwear and her ankles tied together with her shoelaces, with three bullet holes in her head and three in her collarbone.

Sizakele was a well known out lesbian and an HIV activist working for the Positive Women's Network. Whoever murdered her and Salome, who was the mother of a one-year-old baby, knew they were lesbians. Hundred of people crammed into the Ipelegeng Centre and the Mopedi Community Hall for their memorial and funeral services. It was so crowded that I could not get into the hall. I spoke to Sizakele in my heart. I told her I was praying that she should fight and not rest until the people who killed her have been brought to justice.

After the funeral came the Triple Seven Campaign at Constitution Hill. The Campaign was called the Triple Seven Campaign because Sizakele and Salome were murdered on the seventh day of the seventh month in 2007. Hundreds of activists called on the government, religious leaders, traditional leaders, NGOs, politicians, and other stakeholders, including ordinary citizens, to wake up and pay attention to the violence that is happening to gay and lesbian people and to do something to stop it, but the Triple Seven Campaign has its work cut out for it because the violence against lesbians has continued.

Straight men are responsible for the crimes against lesbians. Although we have a Constitution that gives rights to lesbians and gay people that they never had before, there is still so much hatred and prejudice. It is difficult and dangerous for black lesbians in Soweto. Lesbians are contracting HIV because of rape. Men don't accept lesbians. They think they have to teach them a lesson by raping them. They call it "corrective rape." Black lesbians who have been raped say that during rape the rapists insult them, saying things like, "Ja, you! You thought you were a man!" Or, "You are a lesbian because you have never had a great penis!" Men think that if they teach a lesbian how to have sex with a man it will change her behaviour. But will a woman who is raped feel like sleeping with a man? Has being a lesbian got anything to do with men?

It is not about wanting to sleep with men or not wanting to sleep with men. Maybe that is what is so threatening to men. Some men just don't understand that women prefer women. It is ignorance. Men are so ignorant. Part of it is that they are scared. Women are doing things for themselves and men are scared of women being powerful. Women used to depend on their husbands but now men are afraid of women taking their power.

After the murder of Salome and Sizakele, another attack also happened to some women after they were seen at Breeze. The attack against Lash and her friends happened four months after the first attack. In this horrific incident, Lash was shot and recovered, but her friend who was shot died. They had been verbally harassed by some men at Breeze and were driving home when they were attacked. There are no safe lesbian spaces anywhere. There is only one other club in Soweto where lesbians are welcome. It is called Simply Blue but it is really a gay man's spot. The population there is highly gay so in that space you will not really meet other women. There is one lesbian event that is happening in Rosebank, but it is once a month. To go there if you are a lesbian from the township means you must first pay double transport to go to Rosebank, then you must have money for drinks, and when you finish clubbing at 12 at night you must have money for a meter taxi back to the township. It is not easy. That is why lesbians who are looking for fun or to meet people will go to Breeze even though they have heard of all the incidents and they know that lesbians are targeted when they leave the club. If I had my way I would close down the club. Too many people who have been there have died.

I am also the kind of lesbian that is targeted by the men who are raping lesbians. In my dress code and my mannerisms and my attitude I am a butch lesbian. That is the way people see me in the lesbian world. The way I dress makes me feel powerful in myself and it makes me recognisable to other lesbians. I like the fact that there are masculine or butch lesbians because they give lesbians visibility in the township. My ancestor, Nkunzi, also likes me to dress in a manly way. I am not the only lesbian sangoma whose ancestor feels this way. One of the lesbian sangomas interviewed by Busi[1] said, "When I arrived at training they made me wear a skirt. While I was still wearing it another sangoma from outside

---

1 "Busisiwe Kheswa interviewed "Baas Jonn" for GALA

came in and said she was sent to tell me to wear the clothes that I am used to because my grandfather doesn't recognise me like this. My trainer asked what kind of clothes I normally wear and I told her I wear trousers and that is when I came out to her. She called my mother and asked her to bring me some shorts so that I could wear them under the traditional cloths. Then I was given trousers and that is when I became brighter and clearer. It was when my ancestor was more powerful.

I am more protected than other butch lesbians because I am a sangoma and because I am well known in my community but I do sometimes have that fear in me. When I have stayed by myself in my house I find myself thinking, "Do they know that I am by myself?" But for me, I am helped by being a sangoma and there are times when I have been in danger and my ancestor, Nkunzi, has protected me. Once when I was going home and a car approached me and this guy stopped and he said, "Get inside the car!" I refused and he pulled out a knife. I held the knife and it just went through and cut me and left a scar. I fought with this guy. I remember picking him up and smashing him on the windscreen. People came and I went home and cleaned the wound and bandaged it. I had someone in me protecting me and helping me. I think I was supposed to die, but I didn't.

When I moved into my house, I didn't put burglar proofing on the windows. Once, in the middle of the night, I heard something. I was alone and I became scared. Quickly I just thought, let me become naked. I was wearing shorts and a T-shirt, so I just undressed and I took my *phehla* and I had my beads around me. This guy came into the house and it was dark. I stood in the passage and when I could feel he was near me I just switched on the light. The guy who was still outside ran away when I switched on the light. The one who was in the passage looked me and he looked at my hand with my stick in it and without saying anything he quickly ran away. He was so shocked, his mouth was open. His eyes went up and down looking at my naked body and after a few minutes he just ran.

People have that fear in them of what a sangoma will do to them. With me, my trainer taught me to be a healer and to help people, not to use the power I have been given to do bad things to people. I feel like Hlengiwe. When I interviewed her she said, "I feel powerful because in this village I am the only healer who has survived all the witchcraft and I know what I'm doing and I am healing people. That makes me feel powerful."

On the other hand, sangomas are afraid of other sangomas because they know what they can do. A gay guy I interviewed put it like this: "Being a sangoma you get killed. There are others who hate you and then there are others who love you totally. You will never know with people, which one loves you and which one you should help. If you don't look after yourself who is going to? Because they are going to hit you with muthi and at the end we will bury you, so as a sangoma you have to walk steady and you don't have to rush things. If you rush things you'll be hurt."

I don't like to rush. I just do things with respect for people and I expect that respect from people. Right now the guys in the area where I am staying are so respectful of me. They just respect me a lot. After the murder of Sizakele and Salome I protected a young lesbian who was afraid, after she was threatened by neighbourhood men, that the same thing would happen to her as Sizakele and Salome. I took her to stay in my family house with my sister and I told the Meadowlands thugs to protect her and they did. I don't go around being in the corners, standing with those guys. I just pass them and say, "Hi. How are you?" Even them, they like to come to me. They like to talk to me.

Although I am protected as a sangoma, the youth are not balanced these days. There is always a danger that a person may be under the influence of drugs or he may have just given up on life. I am thinking about a young person who says, "I don't have anything to lose. If I kill a sangoma, what do I have to lose?"

If I could have my way, I would hold a huge rally and invite parents of gay children and friends of gay children and members of the public and the police. I would not invite just gay people but everyone together, and I would ask them to join in a march like the women who marched on the Union Buildings, so that with one voice we can shout: "No more! No more!"

CHAPTER ELEVEN

Making Connections

EACH OF MY DIFFERENT ROLES, as a Zulu woman, as a lesbian and as a sangoma, comes with its own challenges. Working at Constitution Hill gives me a high view. I can stand with my back to our apartheid history which is still alive in the Old Fort and the Women's Prison and see the Constitutional Court and be reminded of all that is good in our country; and I can stand on top of the hill outside the Constitutional Court and get an overview of Johannesburg. I can see the good and the bad of the city. This is what I try to do when I think about my own life. I try to take a look from a high place and see the good and the bad.

The stories of the sangomas I interviewed made me feel pity, especially those who told me they couldn't finish up their studies because the ancestors didn't give them a chance. I looked at myself and I saw I was lucky. I had a better trainer who showed me the way and I managed to finish school. Some had to stay in training for years, doing terrible jobs for their trainers because they couldn't pay. There were so many like that. I remember one man named Maguga who was three years in training because of poverty. He was one of the lucky ones because when it was the day for him to receive his healing powers, something amazing happened. People offered to help with different things. Some even popped out R100 and R50 notes. He thought he was going to have a small, cheap goat, but he was surprised. His trainer said it was because of his ancestors.

Others were not so lucky, like one who stayed for four years because there was no money at home. He told me sometimes a trainer can be merciful and talk to the ancestors and release *amathwasa* with no bones or muthi. But for him there was no mercy.

Sangomas don't get clients every day. I have another job, and I don't depend on the money from being a sangoma but for others there is nothing else they can do. Making your life as a sangoma a business is a big mistake. This is one thing I have learned. My trainer told me, "Being a sangoma is not a business, it is being a helper. That is one thing you should know." If I didn't take that up I think I would have ended up like a lot of other sangomas, taking too much money from their trainees or their clients. My trainer told me, "Don't think you will make money as a sangoma. Your job is to help people not to take their money." She said, "Look at me, I am a nurse. I go to work and come back home and help people." Some sangomas, after they train, think this is their whole life. That is not good. My trainer is a nurse and she is working at Orlando Clinic. She is on the dentist's side. She is a dental nurse. She has been there for a long time and they know she is a sangoma.

There are sangomas who will ask for R500 and then they just do something that won't be that helpful, knowing that you are going to come back after three days. And when you come back after three days they will ask for another R300. These sangomas are bringing the name of sangomas down.

Others even say, "Bring a suitcase of R100, 000 and you will get R500, 000 back." That is a lie. How can that be? I can't even make my own 20c to be a 40c, how can I make your R100, 000 into R500, 000? I normally say to them, "Look at me, do you think I have money?" A man asked me for a herb to make him win the lotto. I told him straight, "I don't have the herb to make you win the lotto." I told him, "If you know a sangoma who gives a herb like that, you should go. I don't have that herb. There is no herb to make someone have money."

For me I think it is about how you are raised and how you are trained. My trainer told me, "You can't put money in front of you and put someone's health behind you. Someone's health has to come in front and payment must come last. Even if you don't get paid, you have saved a life." Those words have built me. My mother also raised me with a good attitude to money. She used to say, "Don't look at other people's wealth, build your own wealth and thank God for whatever you have got. Be thankful for what you have got." And then I remember my teacher saying, "There is no such word as "can't". I think these attitudes have built me.

It takes courage to be honest as a sangoma because people want all kinds of things that are not good for them. I remember one woman who wanted me to give her something so that she could hold her husband, like a love potion. I told her, "You can't give your husband this because he will die. In your husband's culture you are not supposed to give a love potion." She thought I was joking and she went to another sangoma and that sangoma gave her a love potion. She came to me on a Sunday. On Wednesday she came back to me and she told me, "My husband has been shot at the complex and he is dead. I should have listened to you." I told her, "You went to another sangoma. There is nothing you can do, he is dead." There are some people who come from a family or a clan that does not allow things like love potions. You are not supposed to give them a love potion or any herbs to control them. It all depends on the ancestors. I warned her, "Your husband came from a culture where you are not supposed to give any herbs." That is what killed him.

When I think of the stories of some of the people I interviewed I think of my mother with gratitude because she accepted me as a lesbian and she made a way for me. Many of the lesbians I interviewed were not accepted. Some were thrown out with nothing.

Now that we have the Civil Union Act and gays and lesbians are allowed to get married legally, it is my dream to get married. If I had money I would buy my girlfriend a ring and ask her to marry me. Although I don't believe in lobola, my girlfriend's parents would want lobola for her and she herself would want me to pay lobola and because I love her, I will do it. But for me lobola is not a good system. I would want to do a ceremony of exchanging cows. It is important for combining the ancestors, so that her ancestors will know me and know that now I am sharing my life with her and my ancestors will know her and they will know that she is sharing her life with me now. If we are together in spirit and sexually, my ancestors should not be surprised to see that she is here all the time, every day, with me. So my ancestors should know about her. This is a way of introducing her to my ancestors, but not by purchasing her. If I paid lobola I would be doing something that I don't agree with and deep down in my heart I won't be feeling all right. I would feel like I have purchased her, I have paid for her like she has a price, like one of my sneakers or a piece of jewellery that I wear. I don't want it like that.

In my relationship with my partner, I believe in being flexible. Sometimes I do take on those man actions of being the head of the house. I believe that when danger comes, I stand first. I protect my partner. She stands behind me and I come first. That is the male responsibility. I do believe that the male partner should be the provider. If I had the money I would provide for her. Nkunzi helps me a lot with male actions. I also express the feminine side of myself in my relationship with my partner. We share cooking and things like making the bed. When I am in Meadowlands, I live a modern life, not a traditional life. My partner calls me her "modern husband."

One thing about me is that I learned from a young age how to love and respect difficult people. First there was my father. He caused me so much pain but when he died, I had forgiven him completely. After my mother died, we found my father staying alone in a shack in Orange Farm. He had full-blown AIDS and we could see that he was dying. My sister, Thuli, said he must come home. First we took him to my grandfather's house but my grandfather couldn't take care of him. Then he came to our mother's house but after a short time it was too difficult for us to look after him so we took him to a hospice near Highgate in Soweto. It was in February 2005.

I visited him there and he asked me to forgive him and to talk to my sisters about forgiving him. He said he was sorry for what he did to us. He was so, so thin. He had sores around his mouth and his private parts. He couldn't eat and he was losing his mind. The colour of his skin changed from black to grayish. His lips were red. He messed himself and he was wearing a nappy. I could see he was feeling ashamed. He felt so ashamed. It was so painful seeing a man who had dignity and respect falling down like that. It was a painful thing. Before he was a strong man with muscles and beautiful big lips and now he couldn't look at me. He was so embarrassed. I prayed, "God, just release him." After he died we buried him in the same cemetery as my mom.

Zulus have a tradition of fighting their way up. Zulu men believe that to be a Zulu you have to be a dictator. You have to oppress and not let anyone oppress you. The males oppress, not the females. The females are just there to look after the house and bear children. I feel more male and powerful, not female. I think it comes with Nkunzi. I never see myself as someone who can fulfill their dream but there is someone in me who pushes me. There is someone who gives me power and courage not to give up. I think this is my male ancestor in me. I believe Nkunzi assists me, pushes me, and helps me.

A Zulu man is supposed to be a breadwinner and look after the family. He stands on his word and his grounds are his grounds, and being the man of the house he makes the rules and decides how everybody must behave. He understands how women must behave, how children should behave and how he should be presented and presents himself to the public. He has a way of presenting himself to the family and a way of presenting himself to the public. Some Zulu men are respected in the public and they don't even smile or talk but at home they are lovable and kind. You can find them playing with the kids or even washing dishes. But in public they are different. In public a Zulu man may be generous and if you ask for ten rand he will give it to you. But at home if his children ask for money he doesn't give it. They are like that, Zulu men. They are two different people.

I could say that I am also two different people. I am a loving person and I have a side that people see and they are surprised. For example, when I play with kids, people say I don't look like somebody who plays with kids. And sometimes I become emotional or even cry and people don't expect me to be emotional. I have a serious side and a side that smiles. I have a male side and a female side. I have a traditional side and a modern side. I am

155

definitely two people.

The Zulu man who was my role model while I was growing up, my uncle Vusumuzi, loves me but still struggles with my same-sex sexuality. I tried to ask him how he feels about my sexuality, to ask him, "Do you accept me?" He ignored me. He just told me to go and fetch him something to eat. Later, when he was drunk, he came to me and said, "I love you the way you are." I asked him, "Why didn't you say it earlier?" He didn't answer but much later in the night when I was standing there with my partner and he passed by, he said, "Is this the girl you are going to pay lobola for?" He was talking in his time, not in my time, not in the time when I wanted an answer from him. I felt somehow he has to tell me he accepts me when he is under the influence of alcohol. I was happy to hear him say he loves me the way I am but I didn't want him to say it under the influence of alcohol. I wanted him to say it in his sober state of mind. The following day, I tried to talk to him and he was pushing me aside. He didn't want to talk to me. He said, "No, no, no, no, no. You are going to put me in jail with all these questions." He is afraid of saying he loves me like I am when he is in his sober state of mind. He can only speak freely when he is under the influence of alcohol.

My life is not only for me, it is also for my ancestor, Nkunzi. When I am about to dance before a ceremony, when I am in my spiritual way, I praise Nkunzi. It is him who is talking, he is praising himself using my body. It is him talking, expressing love for himself.

Abe sekunjalo kakhulu
(Lo! It is now well so)

Abe sengingu Nkunzi Emnyama
(Lo! I am now Black Bull)

Insizwa yakwa Sangweni
(The young man of Sangweni)

Abe sekunjalo kakhulu
(Lo! It is now well so)

Abe sengidabuka ngenjabulo
(Lo! I now originate with joy)

Phezukomsebenzi wama khehla
(Upon the work of men)

Abe sekunjalo kakhulu
(Lo! It is now well so)

Abe sengithanda ukudumisa uyise wami
(Lo! I now love to glorify my father)

Abesengizalwa ngu Elemina
(Lo! I am now born of Elemina)

Insizwa yakwa muNsipa
(The young man of Nsipa)

Abe sekunjalo kakhulu
(Lo! It is now well so)

Abesekuba umkhulu uMahlasela
(Lo! There is now grandfather Mahlasela)

Insizwa Kadumase
(The young man of Dumase)

Abe sekunjalo kakhulu
(Lo! It is now well so)

Abesekuba umkhulu Dungamazi
(Lo! There is now grandfather Dungamazi)

Insizwa kaHlatshwayo
(The young man of Hlatshwayo)

Abe sekunjalo kakhulu
(Lo! It is now well so)

Abese kuba ngugogo Thumba
(Lo! There is now grandmother, Thumba)

Insizwa kaMcobokazi
(The young man of Mcobokazi)

Abe sekunjalo kakhulu
(Lo! It is now well so)

Abesekuba ngugogo Mkhulu Manza
(Lo! There is now great grandmother Manza)

Abese kuba inyoni elimhlophe lihlezi phezu kwamalwandle
(Lo! There is now a white bird sitting upon the oceans)

Abese kuba idada lidabula amanzi ngezimpiko
(Lo! There is now a duck cutting the water with its wings)

Abe sekunjalo kakhulu
(Lo! It is now well so)

Abese ngithanda uku nanazela abanikazi bempande
(Lo! I love to applaud the givers of the root)

Bona abangidabula ikhanda
(They who mend my head)

Bangivula isifuba
(They open my chest)

Ngisho impande ka Majoye
(I say the root of Majoye)

Abesekunjalo kakhulu
(Lo! It is now well so)

Abese ngithanda ukunanazela abanikazi bempande
(Lo! I now love to applaud the givers of the root)

GLOSSARY

amabhayi	cloths that are wound around new sangoma trainees
amacansi	grass mats
amadlozi	ancestors
amathwasa	trainee sangomas (literally, "children of the ancestors")
bliksem	beat someone up (literally, "lightning")
doek	a cloth worn on the head
dompas	reference book (literally, "stupid pass")
Egoli	isiZulu name for Johannesburg (literally, "the City of Gold")
ekuthwaseni	training to be a sangoma
enamo	place where remedies are prepared
endumbshe	working space
hlobongo	thigh sex
ibheshu	apron made of leather, solid at the back and cut into strips at the front
ihwatha	shawl
Ikhamba	African beer
Imbatha	vest made of leather worn by Zulu men for ritual celebrations
imbiza	pot of medicine

Glossary

Impepho	a herb that is burned before communicating with the ancestors
imyalo	rules for living the life of a sangoma
injiti	traditional cloth
Inknyamba	the powerful one
inkohnkoni	a non-offensive term for gay and lesbian people (literally, "Blue Wildebeest")
intombiyebhayi	maiden or virgin
intshomane	the sound of drums beating
inyongo	the gall bladder of a goat
iphande	a branch cut from a tree, anointed with blood and used to indicate that the ancestors are protecting the house
isiphandla	a bracelet made of goat hair
isiqhulo	a tall, traditional hat with a flat top
isiqiki	a tree stump
isithembu	a second wife
istabanes	a contemptuous term for gay and lesbian people which can be broadly translated as "hermaphrodite"
ithambo	the bone from the knee joint of a goat
khalela inkani	a stage during sangoma training (literally, "to cry for stubbornness")
klap	smack
lobola	dowry paid by a Zulu man to the family of his bride
Makhosi	greeting, meaning "the chieftaincy", used by Mnguni sangomas
Mnguni	ancestors from a family line
mteto	a same-sex marriage ceremony in which novices are "married" to veterans

Mundawu	ancestors, not necessarily from a family line
muthi	traditional remedy
Nyankwabe	an ancestral wife
phehla	a sangoma stick
rondavel	a circular house with a thatch roof
sangoma	a traditional Zulu healer
sjamboks	whips, usually made from hide
Thokozani	greeting, meaning "blessed one", used by Mundawu sangomas
tokoloshe/ utokoloshe	an evil spirit
toyi-toying	dancing at a demonstration to show protest
tsotsi	a thug; often a member of a gang; tending to dress showily
tsotsi taal	urban patois
ugogo	grandmother
ukhamba	calabash; a type of gourd
ukuhlolwa	virginity testing
ukushonisa	a ritual to send the ancestors to rest
umkhulu	grandfather
umqhele	crown made from leopard skin
uqhwembe	large bowl

Other titles by Fanele

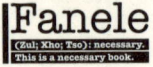

The African Union and Its Institutions
edited by John Akokpari, Angela Ndinga-Muvumba
and Tim Murithi

A Dialogue of the Deaf:
Essays on Africa and The United Nations
edited by Adekeye Adebajo and Helen Scanlon

Human Sexuality in Africa:
Beyond Reproduction
edited by Eleanor Maticka-Tyndale,
Richmond Tiemoko and Paulina Makinwa-Adebusoye

To Have and To Hold:
The Making of Same-Sex Marriage in South Africa
edited by Melanie Judge, Anthony Manion
and Shaun de Waal

Africa's Human Rights Architecture
edited by John Akokpari and Daniel Shea Zimbler

The African Women's Protocol:
Harnessing a Potential Force for Positive Change
by Rosemary Semufumu Mukasa

Other titles by Jacana

A Basket of Leaves:
99 Books that Capture the Spirit of Africa
by Geoff Wisner

African Psycho
by Alain Mabanckou

Khabzela:
The Life and Times of a South African
by Liz McGregor

Bead by Bead
Reviving an Ancient African Tradition:
The Monkeybiz Bead Project
by Barbara Jackson and Kristy Evans

Memory and Magic:
Contemporary Art of the !Xun and Khwe
by Hella Rabbethge-Schiller

Hearing Visions Seeing Voices
by Mmatshilo Motsei

Tommy Boys, Lesbian Men and Ancestral Wives:
Female Same-Sex Practices in Africa
by Ruth Morgan and Saskia Wieringa